Round Bend Press Books

Also by the author:

A Marvelous Paranoia: A Memoir

Four Absurd Plays

Alt-Everything: Essays on History

Nightscape in Empire & the Talent Poems

Cello Music & Other Poems

The Children of Vaughn

Along Came the Death Squad

Cold Eye: A Generation of Voices

Third and a Mile

A Shotgun Diary: The scattered, inconsequential, hyperbolic, rude, tempestuous and dangerously dull journal of an Oregon football fan!

Terry Simons

Round Bend Press Books
Portland, Oregon

All rights reserved. No part of this book may be reproduced in any form by any means electronic or mechanical, including photocopying, recording or by any information storage and retrieval systems, without written permission of the publisher or author except where permitted by law.

Copyright 2018 by Terry Simons

Round Bend Press Books
1115 S.W. 11th Ave.
Portland, Oregon

First Edition

Cover design: Buddy Dooley

ISBN: 978-0-9965266-4-7

American Football—the Oregon Ducks—the Pacific Athletic Conference—College Football—the Pac-12
Published in the USA

roundbendpressbooks.blogspot.com

I am not going to stand up to show pride in a flag for a country that oppresses black people and people of color...

I'm going to continue to stand with the people that are being oppressed.

--Colin Kaepernick

God ain't got nothing to do with winning a damn football game.

--Jim Brown

Introduction

I used to be a big sports nut. I still am to an extent, but not the way I was as a youngster and into my twenties. I think my interest may have dropped off after I quit playing the games. I was disappointed I wasn't good enough to make it all the way to the big leagues in baseball, or the NFL or NBA. So sports lost some sheen for me eventually. At various times it might pick up again, off and on. I still occasionally get absorbed in a World Series or NBA playoffs, for instance.

I played on the line at a small college before giving up football. I got the crap kicked out of me a few times. But I could dish it out, too. I learned how to cheat. An offensive lineman, right guard, I learned how to hold big time. I often got away with it. There's a technique for doing it right. But I do believe refs watch for it more these days. It may not be as easy as it once was.

Here's one thing I've noticed about football. Everybody is bigger now. They're faster too, particularly the really big guys who now run like the little guys when I played.

I have great memories of one particular small college game against Humboldt State in Arcata, going down on a kickoff and hitting a return man so hard the ball flew 20-feet into the air. A teammate picked it off when it came down and strolled into the end zone for an easy defensive TD.

Another time I recovered a teammate's fumble in open space, pulling to the left to block, thought I might score, but I didn't. Everything was in slow motion.

The great athletes talk about that, how time suspends when they're in a "zone." Feels like everything is in front of you,

you're not moving very fast, but you're actually moving very quickly.

Michael Jordon used to talk about that.

Announcers cry, "He's in a zone!" describing a series of great plays by a performer. You've played sports, you know what it is if you've been there.

Well, I was never really in the zone. I was just naturally slow. What I was feeling, the suspension of time, is what everybody saw; it was reality because that is actually what happened.

I couldn't run very fast at all. That's why I played the line at 190 pounds. If I'd had wheels, I could have been a helluva receiver, because I had glue-hands.

So I gave up football for physical reasons.

But I also had other cultural/political reasons for giving up football at that time. I played in the era of dissent. I couldn't identify with the jock mentality, never could really. I just loved the game. I could take or leave most of my football playing friends. Well, not friends, but teammates.

There may have been a few others on that college football team who attended a morning football practice before heading off to the antiwar protest in the afternoon, but I can't remember them.

Eventually, I enrolled at Oregon. These days I still love to watch college football. Oregon is "my dream school."

Terry Simons

MONDAY, DECEMBER 30, 2013

The Withering Noise

This has been a most unpleasant year for me as an Oregon football watcher, and as a college football fan in general.

Oregon vs. Texas tonight in the Alamo Bowl may be my last stand. The timing and symbolism can't be beat.

Something has changed in the game—I should say surrounding it—that has made the entire experience of watching and attempting to enjoy the spectacle and color of college football less agreeable than in the past.

It didn't happen overnight, of course. The game as spectacle has been evolving for a number of years now, but the bottom line for me is that the game no longer gives me the joy it once did. I don't like the new trend. I have turned the other cheek in the main. Perhaps it is time to give up on it altogether.

Its colors have changed, too, like something growing liver spots over time. The game has grown ugly, not on the field where it maintains a certain appeal, but everywhere else.

My relationship with the game is floundering like a bad marriage. We may have irreconcilable differences.

The politics of the game have changed for the worst. The actual bottom line—the economy of the game—has shifted, and I am ill-equipped to deal with its newest shibboleths; in fact, I do not even care about the politics of games or their monetized values.

Never have. That is one reason why I'm not a big NFL fan. Business is business there, and pretty brutal at that. I don't like the seeping fiscal brutality of the college game. It's distasteful.

The college football coach as CEO sounds like a drag, man.

Wins and losses are just that to me—I was a football fan once, not a Wall Street investor with a psychopath's interest in money. I played the game when I was a kid, and for the longest time that carried over for me, probably gave me more cause than most to value the game, at least on a personal level. I understood the things that made the game enjoyable for me, and the least of them were tied to money.

As a player, I won a few and lost a few. Everybody does.

The entertainment value of the game has been usurped by its burgeoning business dimensions. When I think of my life as a kind of anti-corporate shill, a voice in the wilderness you might say, college football no longer meets the criteria with which I measure things of value within my own existence.

In my value system money is way down the list. Success is having a good day as opposed to a miserable one as long as you can keep a roof over your head and eat once or twice a day.

I'm not particularly enamored of CEOs. I've met a few, and I might say we seldom see eye-to-eye about the meaning of life, much less the price of a widget, doodad, or gizmo.

College football is now reflective of a corporate mentality that guides too much in American society these days. Call it my weariness of the propensity people have for judgment or grandiosity when reflected through the prism of money. Call it corporate codification, or the will to marginalization, for that is what corporations are best at—marginalizing people who don't fit in.

Call it another unfortunate consequence of the modern, technological world. Call it reality. Call it whatever you like, just don't try to convince me that games are life and death—or that business ought to define their principal meaning.

That stuff never interested me. Today it is in your face. Here's what Joe makes. Is he any good?

I once worked in the health care industry. Now that was a life and death environment. I made a living as a corporate propagandist, writing hopeful tracts on the "services" and "medical advances" and the supposed wonderfulness of the ugly place that surrounded me daily.

Here's what made it ugly—the bottom line. The greed I witnessed in that place was of the same kind you see everywhere now. I left to pursue a less damaging lie.

Halliburton and Dick Cheney had nothing on my old employer, folks.

You could say it wasn't actually life affirming.

I may leave college ball behind because it has become a damnable lie. It's causing more damage to me personally than I'm comfortable with enduring. Its hypocrisies have overwhelmed me.

I never thought I'd witness a time when a 10-2 Oregon team would be run through with a rapier by so many hacks in the media and so many delusional fans that you might imagine should be happy that it is no longer the seventies in Eugene.

To say I was shocked by the vitriol that arose after Oregon's two losses this year would be putting it mildly. I didn't see it coming, perhaps because I never expected Oregon to be as good as it is in the first place.

People talk about the sense of entitlement the players seem to have at Oregon as the spoiled progeny of big bad Nike. It has occurred to me that a worse problem lies with the average Oregon fan. Now losing is cause to complain about everything.

The seventies in Eugene are a part of the historical record, and I liked it better back then. But that doesn't make me modern enough, I guess. The object has become to kill the coach, so to speak and to cry over two losses.

Good lord...

I may be losing my love of college ball. It happens. I can't deal with the disappointment of my fellow Ducks. Their disappointment disappoints me.

"Well, it should have been a better year," they cry.

Well, in my opinion everything should be better, but that doesn't make me an expert.

To the gasbags who want change and change now in the Oregon football program, I say this: quit blaming others for your miseries. Quit blaming kids, age 18 to 21, for your unhappiness, your illusions. You'll never cast away all of your miseries to begin with. You sound ludicrous.

The kids aren't listening to you anyway. Hell, in most cases you don't even know them. You don't seem to care if they're good students, nor are you interested in their academic lives. All you are interested in is the glory that you seem to believe will be reflected on your life if Oregon is great.

That is not the way things work.

Oregon enjoyed a great run under Chip Kelly. The unfortunate backlash to his success is that Oregon is now defined by his shadow. I have news for everybody who hasn't noticed. Kelly is long gone.

He ain't coming back, either. With the success he's had this year in Philly, he'll likely be out of college ball for a long time, too.

O, how long will this persist? And must it really?

I liken the present situation at Oregon to what happened at UCLA when the great basketball coach John Wooden retired.

Everybody who came along after him was treated like crap. Some of them were actually pretty good coaches, too.

But they didn't last long, not amid the dumb, withering noise.

I have one piece of advice for anybody who can't stand the thought of ever witnessing a loss on the old gridiron, be it at Oregon or somewhere else.

Grow up. It does happen and the longer you dwell on it the more obnoxious you sound.

I, as much as anyone, hope for the best from Oregon football going forward. I'm not going to kid myself into believing that I have any say in what happens next, however.

You know, the All-American quarterback might get hurt or something.

FRIDAY, AUGUST 2, 2013

Shoot the Muralist!

Because you're dying to know, I'll tell you my thoughts on the new Football Psyops Center at the University of Oregon (Hatfield-Dowlin Complex).

(This isn't a statement about what football is or isn't relative to academia. That is another issue, and frankly I am tired of it. If people gave a fuck about education in this country it would be less expensive than it is now. In any case, I believe what you get out of education is what you put into it; if that means being an autodidact or coming up empty, so be it.)

The building is a $70 million abomination, albeit a beautiful abomination, at least on the outside, where its lines are superb. In that regard it is a magnificent work of art.

But that is where its beauty ends and, unfortunately, poor taste takes over. Because I don't believe football was ever designed to be a frilly thing, the frills inside this building are comical.

On the inside the building is a garish travesty that highlights the bad taste often associated with ostentatious displays of wealth and fashion. Think of all the assembly-line paintings you'll find inside the corporate offices of a multinational insurance company, where the receptionist wears a beehive coif and the CEO looks like Donald Trump in a bad tie.

It's like that.

Its interior has the quality of a badly curated museum. Its tawdry affectations betray an empty-headed consumerism, kitsch, and paint-by-numbers design.

Striving for edginess, it came out mundane.

Even the rugs are ugly.

If I were the architect I'd be pissed because a team of idiotic interior designers ruined my perfectly beautiful masterpiece. At least he didn't acquiesce to placing a big yellow O on the facade, though I'm sure somebody would have thought that a good idea.

The building is overkill, but it is overkill in ways that you may not appreciate. College football as a corporate endeavor entered the pantheon of excess long ago. With that comes the misbegotten hubris associated with this building, the equivalent of a Napoleon Complex.

It's silly.

"Over-the-top" isn't a good enough phrase for this stinker.

If I didn't like football, i.e., care for the game rather than its accouterments, I'd pooh-pah the whole deal, like many critics indeed have.

In fact I am likely not alone thinking this—the chances are Oregon's football team, coddled as it is, will forget to come to play a few times this season.

The first time a team comes into Eugene and dresses on the bus before slipping out of Autzen with an upset because a few Oregon players couldn't pull themselves out of the players' lounge in time for kickoff—that'll be the day we acknowledge the truth:

The Oregon Football Psyops Center is a joke, and the over-marketing of the Oregon brand is embarrassing.

FRIDAY, DECEMBER 28, 2012

Lache is Not Great

Texas is renowned for its high school and college football programs.

In literature, film, and the everyday churn of journalistic bombast the record is clear on this. Texas is a football factory, a landscape dominated by its varieties of sage brush, open space and football-generated mythology.

A cursory glance at the history of Texas football is replete with heroes and anti-heroes, and because this is America that mythology is transcendent.

You don't think G.W. Bush escaped to his "ranch" in Texas with regularity during his presidency to mull over the big questions of world leadership, do you?

Of course not. He went home frequently to commune with the ghosts of football's past, to revel in the myth.

Decked out in his finest dude-ranching gear, playing for the camera like an arrogant pass-catching god who has just scored his team's winning touchdown in the big game, he even spiked his pitchfork like a football, thinking perhaps of one of his heroes scoring yet again.

Preening, speaking in the broken, Texas-invented idiom of grunts and monosyllabic poetry that defines the self-centered jock, Bush sought succor in the myth—we're good, we're damn good, and this is the championship season.

He is gone fortunately, having wrecked everything, but Texas football persists.

This is why I badly want to see Oregon State crush Texas tomorrow in the Alamo Bowl, brought to you by some corporation or another whose name I've momentarily forgotten.

I can still recall a sweet moment 12-years removed, when Oregon beat Texas in the Holiday Bowl. That little throwback play to a stumbling Joey Harrington was a thing of ugly beauty.

Joey could not run, but he is an Oregonian through and through. That counts.

Let me tell you something about Texas football players. They are only great in my book when they leave Texas and come to Oregon to play their college ball, like Quizz and James Rodgers, one-time stars at OSU.

Or like LaMichael James, Darron Thomas, Josh Huff, Bralon Addison, Chance Allen and the Amoaka brothers. Past, current, and future stars at the University of Oregon.

Lache Seastrunk, the toast of Temple, was great once, when he played at Oregon (or sat behind a bevy of better backs), but now that he plays for Baylor he reminds me of a lesser god.

The young feller helped Baylor crush UCLA last night, but that doesn't make him great, does it? After all, he abandoned Oregon.

Lache could have been a star.

Now he is preening on the sidelines like old George used to do, pointing at the other God in the sky and calling this abomination destiny.

God had a plan all right, that you should take your arrogance home silly Lache.

So this brings me to OSU's Storm Woods. I like him. Seems like a solid kid because he's toughing it out here in rainy Oregon.

He's from Texas, ya'll know? Like Lache and LaMike, he got homesick that first year.

Unlike Lache he didn't run home to Grandma when he wanted to cry.

MONDAY, AUGUST 8, 2011

Life Begins Today

It's that time of year when I get all banged up and sore and break a sweat just by anticipating the excitement, the pageantry, the beautiful, controlled violence of the game of college football.

I am the world's greatest college football fan.

Oregon takes to the practice field today at 1 p.m. to begin preparing for its tough opening game against LSU on Sept. 3 in Dallas, Texas.

Texas is Willie Lyles' territory, as all my football-loving friends know. If you haven't heard about Lyles and his relationship with Oregon's coach Chip Kelly, go back to reading your recent Round Bend Press acquisition and ignore this post.

Oregon players LaMichael James, Darron Thomas, Lache Seastrunk, Josh Huff, Blake Cantu and Anthony Wallace are all from Texas. A tight group, all snatched away from the many second-rate academic institutions that dot that godforsaken state's bleak landscape, enticed by the opportunity to get a solid education and win a shitload of college football games.

They are Oregon heroes who came west to play in the game's greatest conference, the Pac-12.

Texa$$... (Spit!)

I'm a big Duck fan, of course. I went to school in Eugene and have had a long love affair with the team. When I attended classes there in the early seventies Oregon had some very fine football players, but not nearly as many as now.

I sat next to Dan Fouts in poli-sci classes all the time; passed him notes with diagrammed plays I wanted him to try in the next big game.

He said to me one time, smiling at my poorly drawn guaranteed TD, "Simons, you are an idiot to think this will work against USC!"

Hmm...

Well, I can't get down to Eugene to watch my number one team practice, so yesterday I went the second best route available to me. I hiked the four blocks to Portland State's campus and watched my second favorite college team's first practice.

The Mighty PSU Vikings, who unfortunately won only two games last season.

You see, I'm also a proud graduate of PSU, and I have more school spirit to go around than a high school cheerleader.

PSU opens on Sept. 3, too, a game the smart people over at the university decided to reschedule for 1 p.m. to avoid conflict with the televised Duck game at 5 p.m.

Smart move. I'll go to Jeld-Wen to watch my Vikings before I head over to the bar to watch my Ducks.

I have my life figured out for Sept. 3, at least.

And I have some good news for you if you've read this far and give a fuck. PSU will have a much improved team this year—much, much improved. The Jerry Glanville era, a mistake two years removed, is officially and finally over.

Second-year coach Nigel Burton, a (here I clear my throat and grimace) Washington grad, has recruited some massive, mobile linemen from the JC ranks, sprinkled in a few transfers from major programs, and brought aboard some outstanding freshmen to, as the sports jocks on the radio say, "git 'er done."

The Vikings open against Southern Oregon. I played football at Southern Oregon—one year, back in 1970. Strictly small time football. PSU will kill them.

Nigel Burton can recruit, just like Chip Kelly, but with perhaps fewer, er, disposable dollars in hand.

FRIDAY, JUNE 7, 2013

Shared Award/Oregon and the NCAA

It sounds like the NCAA is drawing closer to a decision, finally, regarding Oregon's football program.

I expect the news to be bad, worse than a lot of die-hard Duck fans imagine.

The sin was egregious, to say the least. Oregon's Chip Kelly, now the coach of the Philadelphia Eagles, paid one Willie Lyles, a Houston-based college football talent scout, 25K for a recruiting "package" which materialized in the form of a highly-coveted recruit/running back out of Texas named Lache Seastrunk.

Seastrunk never played a down at Oregon before transferring to Baylor, near his hometown of Temple, where he has become a star and potential Heisman candidate. For the record, Seastrunk and Lyles, who were close before this business began, have both denied that the payment in any fashion influenced the running back's decision to come to Oregon. But the claim is thinly veiled, which is one reason a judgment on this case has taken so long.

The absurdity inherent in this situation is that Kelly and Oregon's compliance office (being the entity that interprets and supposedly abides by the NCAA's rules) never tried to conceal the payment, as it fell in the hazy category of "recruiting services" that many college football programs rely on to find recruits.

Oregon cut Lyles a fat check, too fat as it turned out. Oregon in effect out-bid other colleges who recruited Seastrunk, though the NCAA hasn't been able to unequivocally prove as much.

There is plausible deniability everywhere, in other words.

The typical cost of a package of recruiting information, even in Willie Lyles' orbit of business, was 5K. The 25K check threw up red flags throughout the college football world. In fact, Oregon never received a recruiting package from Lyles, until after questions arose about the deal.

What finally arrived after the fact was a hastily drawn package of outdated and useless material.

Kelly without question took advantage of a gray area in the NCAA guidelines.

He stepped over the line, and essentially embarrassed the powers-that-be in Indianapolis, where the NCAA holds shop and controls the purse strings of the gazillion dollar business of college football.

I expect the NCAA to make an example of Oregon even as it attempts to rewrite the rules governing recruiting services like the one Lyles ran.

Well done.

WEDNESDAY, OCTOBER 5, 2016

The Cleverly Inane

Oregon football is having a down year, much like those I remember well from my adolescence and college-years in Eugene in the last century.

Oregon has been decent for the past 20-years, since "The Pick," which is, in football years, not that long ago. There's lore behind it, which I won't get into because everyone else already has.

The losing bothers the ignorant, though it hasn't much to do with anything important.

It's driving some Oregon fans over the edge, even though it was entirely predictable based on the proven logic of the cyclical in sports. Programs rise and fall, like empires in general. They rise again and fall—like a lullaby.

The head coach is taking most of the heat, but the truth is there's plenty of blame to go around for Oregon's dip.

A larger point is that there are plenty of dip-sticks in Oregon's fan base now, just as there are surrounding every major college program these days.

In my day there was nothing to cheer about with Oregon football, except for the pure pleasure of being in the stadium and watching a college football game—no record of achievement to mourn in passing, just solid ineptitude year after year.

So there was never any cause to go crazy about current events, mounting losses, the end of football history!

Kind of like politics yesterday and today, there's a record of nastiness on the books.

A while back a national writer, whose name escapes me, perhaps George Schroeder of *USA Today*, compared Oregon's program to a Ferrari, the sleek, expensive auto.

That was "clever"—if typically overblown—sports writing, but now people have taken to claiming the car has crashed. It's become a cliché, of course, an easy metaphor to extend to the inane.

Here's a post from a Duck fan at the CBS 247 Sports affiliate, *Duck Territory,* wherein the contributor sees it about like I do:

Super necessary thread. I also hope someone uses the car analogy again for the 1500th time. It's super clever.

But....if we are using the car analogy let's at least be accurate. He was given the keys to a Ferrari and drove that Ferrari as fast he could for two years. The third year the Ferrari got damaged in a wreck and none of his mechanics had the right parts to get the car back on the road immediately, but once the part came in he was back driving that Ferrari as fast it would go, right up until that damn part failed again. In his fourth year of ownership, he hired some new mechanics hoping he could keep the Ferrari on the road, well the parts keep breaking and the most important part, the one that kept breaking last year, is on recall so he had to get a refurbished part and it just doesn't provide the same ride.

It turns out he wasn't being a very good car owner though and wasn't taking it in for regular maintenance or using the right fuel. The front end is now shot, and the rear differential is out of balance.

Now the car is broken down and will be expensive to fix.

Anybody sick of the car analogy yet?

Good job "Duckwad" at Oregon 247!

TUESDAY, DECEMBER 7, 2010

114 Years Later

Like Jerry Allen, in his now famous call of the Civil War game on Saturday, said: Oregon fans have waited 114 years for "this day." That is, entry into the national championship college football game.

In his excitement, Jerry Allen started to sob and lost track of reality. Oregon football fans can't blame him.

Nobody alive can actually remember the first football game between the University of Oregon and Oregon Agricultural College, now OSU, 114 years ago.

But I won't forget this year's 114 years from now, that is for sure. I am overjoyed that Oregon has finally done it.

The season shocked me, yet it didn't really surprise me. I knew how good James and Barner could be, and I liked the experience of the O-line. I looked at the schedule and saw a few stumbling blocks before the season. They would face USC on the road and a tough Stanford team as well as the always dangerous Cal Bears in Berkeley, where Oregon hadn't won in years.

Oregon State in Corvallis? Yikes!

When Jeremiah Masoli did something really stupid, I said, uh oh...so much for the Rose Bowl repeat. When he was kicked off the team, I thought winning eight games behind the play of Nate Costa might be possible.

Darron Thomas? No matter how talented a kid is he has to have experience. Costa had a bit more; I thought Costa was the guy, bad knees and all.

I didn't have an insider's perspective, of course, and Thomas got the call from the coaching staff.

Early in the season Thomas really zipped the ball around and I suspect by now his arm is very tired, which may explain why he didn't bother to pass much late in the season, along with the success of the ground game.

When Barner got hurt I expected James to take on too much, and he did. In the final game, Barner was the better Oregon running back. I expect James to recover, however, regain his legs and be fresh for Auburn. I expect James will star in the big game, no matter its final outcome.

Barner will have his moments as well, as will Thomas.

Alas, as the season wore on, and particularly after Oregon beat USC in Los Angeles, I realized the Ducks had a shot.

They did it, went 12-0 and earned the right to play in the national championship game, also known as the Tostitos BCS Bowl, in Glendale, January 10.

I look forward to the game. But I can tell you right know it will take a Herculean effort to keep Cam Newton down.

The guy is the best football player I've ever seen, and I've watched college football closely for 114 years, just like your average Oregon fan.

SUNDAY, AUGUST 10, 2014

Eyes on Eugene

This would have been the year to write an insider's story following the Oregon Ducks throughout the season.

Maybe someone will.

I'm thinking of two of my favorite sports-related books from years past: David Halberstam's *The Breaks of the Game*, a chronicle of the Portland Trailblazers following their 1977 NBA title, and George Plimpton's *Paper Lion*, the hilarious account of the author's brief, satirical attempt to play quarterback for the Detroit Lions in 1963.

Some things that would make this year's story about Oregon football interesting include the dynamic play and leadership of All-Americans Marcus Mariota, Hroniss Grasu and Ifo Ekpre-Olomu. All three turned down surefire NFL money to return to Oregon for a final run at college ball.

In this day that is in itself remarkable.

Another angle is the tension inherent in the program as second-year coach Mark Helfrich, an Oregonian from Coos Bay, attempts to solidify his coaching career in the long shadow cast by Chip Kelly, who led the team to unprecedented success before moving on to the NFL.

Kelly has been deified in some circles, though people tend to forget that he lost a number of "big games."

Many critics find Helfrich lacking, inasmuch as this is his first head coaching position and he was perceived as shaky last year, leading the Ducks to an 11-2 record.

The second-year coach is on the hot seat, one heated by the imaginations of a rabid fan base. So are offensive coordinator Scott Frost and first-year defensive coordinator Don Pellum.

Last year's record would please most fan bases around the country, but Oregon, behind the money of Nike and Phil Knight, is unique—or thinks it is in many cases. Helfrich is in an unenviable situation.

Unfortunately, Oregon is either going to make it to the new College Football Playoff this season or people are going to demand the coach's ouster. Not fair, but such is the twisted nature of the college football beast now—at least in Oregon.

That's a weird story, telling in its primal "win-at-any-cost" mantra. It should be documented close-up, along with the personalities that shape the team. This is a big football story steeped in a morality play about the direction of college sports.

There are some interesting cats at Oregon right now. Bright guys like Tyler Johnstone and Bralon Addison (who are both out for the season) and preternaturally gifted players like Mariota, Thomas Tyner and the new kid, Royce Freeman, who will soon be a household name.

There are some animals. Jake Fisher is a prime example, a big tackle that plays with nearly unhinged violence.

There is a boatload of emerging athletes, possibly stars, including the fastest high-hurdler in the U.S., Devon Allen.

Oregon has some monster players, a roster as gifted as any other in the league. What does the future hold?

Can the center hold on what many believe is Oregon's last chance to win it all, carried to the promised land by the magnificent, generational QB Mariota? Because UCLA, USC, virtually all the usual heavyweights, are bouncing back and Stanford has had Oregon's number the past two seasons.

There are so many "ifs" one cannot help but be caught up in them—legions of Oregon watchers, here and around the country are curious.

SUNDAY, NOVEMBER 28, 2010

Not Quite There

I hate bandwagon fans.

I watched the Oregon/Arizona game in a local pub Friday evening and an idiot sat down beside me. He wanted to talk a little football, evidently.

He told me his kids attended Oregon, so he's a big Duck fan. He asked me if I thought Oregon could win the National Championship.

I gave my standard answer with the usual bushel of caveats. "Well, there's Auburn, and TCU and Boise State (at the time), and you know, it's difficult to say. But I hope so."

"So, who does Oregon play after this," the guy said, and I thought he was joking.

"Funny guy," I said.

"Well, who do they play next? I just follow Oregon. I don't follow any other teams. Which teams do you follow?"

"I follow football, college football; it's bigger than just Oregon."

"I'm not interested in anybody except Oregon. My kids went there. They love Oregon. So, who's your team?"

"That would be Oregon."

"Well, my kids...."

"Yes, your kids attended Oregon."

"They're big fans."

"Smart kids."

"So, who does Oregon play next?"

"That would be Oregon State."

"Are they any good?"

"I don't know. I don't think anyone knows."

"I just follow Oregon. I'm not interested in Oregon State. Are they a good team?"

"Well, they're not Auburn."

"Auburn?"

"Yes, the second ranked team in the BCS. You know?"

"No, I just follow the Ducks."

"Well, there is more to the game than just the Ducks."

An uncomfortable silence followed as I sipped my beer and tried to listen to the pregame chatter coming from the television over the bar.

"So, who is Oregon playing tonight?" my drinking buddy asked.

"I don't know. I just follow Oregon," I said, and moved to another bar stool.

SUNDAY, NOVEMBER 24, 2013

Send in the Clowns

The fallout from Oregon's unfortunate 42-16 loss to Arizona yesterday in Tucson is yet another example of how expectations leapfrog reality for a large segment of the Ducks' fan base.

Oregon's fans are of two types—the long-suffering fans like me who appreciate reality when they see it and a cadre of "bandwagon" fans steeped in arrogance and a completely unrealistic view of college football and what they think ought to be happening on the field at any given moment.

Fans are dilettantish, and most of them are ignorant.

The bandwagon is in a full-on attack mode now, going so far as to call for a wholesale coaching change in Eugene. Talk about misplaced priorities and an unrealistic view...the new coach is 9-2 in his first season.

Talk to me next year if he's 2-9 and I might support your facile reasoning. Short of turning a blind eye to pedophilia, a football coach is not fired at 9-2, particularly at Oregon, where winning is still new and an entire long-term staff has contributed to the team's recent success.

Helfrich gets next year if he wants it, despite your reckless stupidity. In other words, it is way too early to pin two losses on a failed culture at Oregon. It is way too early to claim Helfrich is a bad coach. It is way too early to say anything other than keep playing and showing effort.

I confess, I do not understand this kind of reactionary nonsense. First, coaches make mistakes just like everybody else, and it is never a given that the coaching has failed simply because a team loses. Did Helfrich and company really make that many mistakes yesterday? I don't see that they did. How can you say it is the coach's fault when a player muffs a pass on the sideline and it falls into a defender's hand, killing a game opening drive, as happened yesterday in Tucson?

Was it a vanilla call? The quick out to a good receiver like Bralon Addison is an Oregon staple, and has been for years. I question anybody who thinks Addison is an entitled ass—good lord, he's an excellent competitor, which you would know if you've been paying attention to the team this year.

He did not make the catch, got it?

Coaches are given way too much credit when a team wins, and way too much blame when it loses.

That realization is lost on the bandwagoneers, most of who have never been in a football game with 70K howling fans giving you the razz from the opening whistle. If you don't know by now that everyone gives Oregon its best shot and has for years, you're missing the subtlety of the game, the very essence of competitive sport at its highest level.

You're missing the point of just how good Oregon has been for five seasons.

Where was Oregon's defense throughout the day? I'll tell you where. Three of the best linebackers Oregon has ever had, the starters from the past three seasons who were the heart of the Ducks' defense, are in the NFL. The guys playing in their stead are nowhere near as good as those three—face reality.

Don't tell me these undermanned, undersized players weren't trying. I won't buy it. I saw too many good plays by this group that transcended its inherent skill level. I also saw a great runner shred Oregon's defense behind excellent blocking.

Despite that, I saw too many effort plays by Oregon to buy what you're selling. Tell me that Chip Kelly left the cupboard bare at linebacker before going to Philly and you might be closer to the truth.

On Oregon's second drive, after the initial epic failure of the defense to stop Ka'Deem Carey, the country's leading rusher, De'Anthony Thomas dropped a pass that would have moved the chains. Is this the first pass Thomas has dropped in his career at Oregon?

I don't think so. Over a career that has seen the little guy do more good than harm to the Oregon team, I'm not going to pin this loss on Thomas' attitude, or that singular drop. Thomas is an exceptionally good player, and when he speaks about his expectations for himself and his team he is speaking honestly. The Ducks would not be where they are/were if Thomas had chosen USC over Oregon as he initially planned—be realistic.

If you want tempered, automatic and pleasing responses from young people you're unrealistic. If Oregon's players offended you by counting their chickens before they hatched, then some fans were even worse offenders.

I've never heard so much bullshit talk about a national championship before the season even started. The players weren't talking about it, though they may have believed it. The fans were doing the talking; the players were striving to succeed.

Thomas did not have a bad day all in all yesterday, other than his drop. He didn't play like a guy who has mailed it in. He ran possessed and gave it his all, including making a one-handed circus catch near the goal line that set up an Oregon score.

That doesn't matter because, you know, Oregon can't stop a run up the middle. This is Thomas' fault? Give me a break.

This is Josh Huff's fault because he is heartbroken for not making it back to the NCG? God forbid that Huff shows a human side and expresses disappointment in a season that turned bad in Palo Alto.

Huff is not an automaton, believe it or not, and if you've never had a dream crushed you're unique. To top it off, Huff was a major reason Oregon got to the NCG versus Auburn three years ago when he played as a true freshman on an unbeaten team. Why shouldn't his expectations as a player be high?

Oregon, particularly Thomas and Huff, did not quit yesterday, except in the minds of those whose own expectations ignore reality. Oregon was beaten by a team with better talent overall, particularly on both lines.

But tell this to the unrealistic fan and he'll try to run you out of the room.

Here's the reality, folks. Oregon wasn't better than Arizona yesterday, nor was it better than Stanford two weeks ago. The Ducks lost because they aren't who some people-- namely the unrealistic—thought they were.

They weren't who they thought they were, either. If you don't think they know that now you're nuts.

The game is played on both lines in a bubble of hand-to-hand fighting. You've never been in a fight if you don't know that, and you've certainly never played the game.

And if you haven't been in a fight, even lost a few, you have no room to talk.

THURSDAY, DECEMBER 1, 2011

Watch Out!

The entire situation has me worried.

No, no, no, not the trickle-down theory that is Round Bend Press (the world will catch up one day), but rather the Pac-12 Championship game, sponsored by UPS and Dr. Pepper (gag me with too much sugar or whatever it is that makes that soft drink product so wretched).

Gag me again because I am about tired of the corporate sponsorship philosophy, even if it is a more realistic view of the world than my own...

No, the football game between UCLA and Oregon set for Eugene tomorrow night gives me pause.

Few people are giving UCLA a chance, and that makes me uncomfortable. With all the distractions surrounding this matchup, I'm hoping Oregon doesn't get lost in the sea-swell of hype (or lampooning) that has dominated the sport's discourse leading up to the game.

Oregon was lost in the hype last month when USC played in Autzen, the supposed loudest stadium in the land, which became very quiet for some reason. Standing on the sideline during that game was a gaggle of NBA stars team-President Phil Knight brought to the game just for fun.

It was a show of shows.

That little gambit cost Oregon; I'm convinced, though one can't conjure empirical evidence on the matter. It appeared to me that the Oregon players were more interested in gathering autographs than touchdowns for three quarters.

This week, Oregon can't even practice inside the football stadium. UPS and Dr. Pepper have colluded with PAC officials to make over the Autzen interior in their images.

Football players would be in the way of the advertising drones.

Good lord, will there be a football game Friday night or a convention of UPS and Dr. Pepper super salesmen?

Oregon is favored by 30, but give me a break. Last I looked UCLA is not a team of 2011 Pop Warner All-Stars. It has big, fast kids (and a few men) on its roster. They landed at the L.A. school for a reason after all. They earned scholarships because at some point in their football careers they could play the game and play it at a high level.

Oregon better push the distractions aside this week, unlike that evening last month when Dwayne Wade tried to talk Chip Kelly into playing quarterback for a series and Kelly almost caved in.

UCLA's players are gonna come out and play hard for their lame-duck coach, Rick Neuheisel.

Money can't buy that kind of emotion.

I think I'll go to the betting parlor today and put money on the Bruins to cover.

SATURDAY, JANUARY 11, 2014

Stupid Rich Fan

A couple of weeks ago when I was feeling low about the state of the typical Oregon football fan and college football in general I argued that many of Oregon's fans are complete morons.

Nothing new there, I guess, but I was having a bad day.

Today, this comment appeared at one of the Oregon fan sites regarding the rumor that long-time Oregon assistant Don Pellum, who played football at Oregon and is responsible for recruiting some of the best linebackers Oregon has ever had, will be promoted to Nick Aliotti's old job as Defensive Coordinator:

I'm sorry but when we are told 'Oregon will spare no expense in making the right hire' and then we don't even promote the best coach on our own staff I can bitch all I want, especially when I contribute money to the athletic department.

Rich, stupid Oregon "fan" found. Case closed.

A rare fan with the balls to tell the above idiot off:

Lmao....you sound like that ridiculous Texas booster. Get over yourself.

SUNDAY, MARCH 23, 2014

A Post-Mortem on Nike U.

The Duck bashers are out in full force on the interweb.

Who are these people? What makes them so vicious?

I doubt if it's much different anywhere in the land, but I just don't understand the negativity people manage to dredge up when their team loses. Or the chortling.

This is the part of sport I can't take—the blame game.

The naysayers are blaming Oregon's excellent and proven coach Dana Altman, the players, the officials, the cheerleaders and the bus driver for the loss last night.

Oh, and Nike.

Right, everyone is to blame, except Wisconsin, which happens to be a very good team that adjusted in the second-half and took advantage of its length to exploit Oregon's undersized and slow front line.

Great coaching there. If you didn't notice Oregon's front court crew was lacking all season you weren't paying attention.

Wisconsin noticed, that is for sure, if belatedly.

That's basketball.

When Oregon adjusted, or tried to, and packed the middle to stop Wisky's inside game, the back court suddenly had open opportunities, which they cashed in like a bundle of overtime bonus checks. That team could flat-out shoot it.

That's not the narrative though in the minds of certain types. The naysayers seem to be more interested in social science and psychology—bless you Harry Edwards, wherever you are. Thank you as well, Ivan Pavlov, wherever you are.

John Canzano walks into the Oregon locker room and, surprise, sees frowny faces. This bugs him, just as the smiley faces Oregon displayed in a football loss to Stanford this season bugged him. You would guess this is his first college rodeo. He can't decide what he wants--calzone or pizza?--in the buffet line.

Hey, JC, the players were pissed in both cases, and could give a damn what you think. Reactions to losing are as varied as the humans who have them. Wasn't last night a sign they cared? I mean, come now, you were critical when a couple of Ducks showed a seemingly cavalier attitude in the Stanford football game and didn't appear to take the thumping to heart.

Those self-defensive and embarrassed smiles on the sideline were deplorable! A true sign of not giving a damn! Right?

Which is it? Be sad or be glad when you lose? Hmm...The dilemma appears to be how to react to losing—a sticky-wicket open to interpretation. We can agree that acting out, picking a fight, is bad form. After that words, if not fists, commonly fly. Though I agree we all need to be nicer to each other, sometimes it just doesn't work that way.

Somewhere in the ether there exists a reaction to a loss that Canzano must envision as proper, a method of dispelling heartbreak. It would be neutral, emotionless, cold, and something other than honesty and the truth of the moment would need to play out.

Would it be like an NFL or NBA locker room, where an outrageous salary for the night's work might salve the wounds? Or would it be more like sitting in front of a keyboard and making shit up?

Who knows?

Oregon wasn't a "team?" Bullshit again. Were they immature? Must be, because only the writers and naysayers have maturity, obviously.

Oregon was a team with an inferior front line. There's no need to rip the players about that. Anyone with an ounce of acumen should be able to admit that without blaming the loss on phantoms. Oregon wasn't going to win it all--by losing in the round of 32 the team is fair game for the writers and would-be pundits/coaches. To hear JC, this loss was all Oregon. Wisconsin had nothing to do with it—except they had a better team on this night.

Take it from a guy who has played on a few losing teams—me. Great guys co-existed on those teams, with a few exceptions. The few bad guys didn't cause the teams to lose. A lack of size, speed and fundamentals did.

Good lord, get real...social relativism is a canard in sports most of the time. Feel-good stories about championship seasons, wherein a team of angels defeats the forces of darkness, are baloney.

Even the state champ has a dickhead on the team. Always.

It's embarrassing to be an Oregon fan at times, given the odd and hilarious paradox in Oregon athletics now. The thinking goes like this: Nike adversely coddles Oregon's players, which causes them to lose big games and act out. Or...Nike coddles them, which means they should never lose while acting out.

Win and it's on Nike. Lose and it's on Nike. The hue and cry is astonishing. The middle ground, good sense, realism, has vanished. You know, because athletes act out, good and bad. You know, because that always happens and always has. Always will.

In a recent year, an athlete on Harvard's much lauded team was kicked out of school for cheating. Damn entitled punk.

Oregon took its loss hard. Would you expect them to take it any other way? If the players cracked a smile, they'd get ripped for that.

But nobody is taking this loss as hard as the fans who expect Oregon to win because it's Nike U, or those who think Oregon lost because it's Nike U.

Christ, it was a game between two decent teams, both of which have corporate backers and, most certainly, a bad egg or two.

Would you like some corporate cheese atop those rotten eggs...?

Short of some kind of national championship outside of track and field (which is miraculously unaffiliated with the famed running shoe company, ha ha) nothing will please the bandwagon fans--except when something pleases them.

Darn it. I wish Oregon wasn't filled with so many bums. I wish they'd take their beatings like real men. I wish Nike would go away and we could have something else to blame.

You know, like other teams' fans do...

MONDAY, SEPTEMBER 11, 2017

Team Identity

The Oregon Ducks are a sensational story now in the college football world as pundits and ordinary fans attempt to figure the team out after two wins—an expected blowout of Southern Utah, and a bizarre victory over an evenly matched Nebraska team.

The Nebraska game was bizarre because of the way it played out in two halves of vastly different styles of football—fast and sluggish.

A first half that conjured memories of the hyper-frenetic Ducks under Chip Kelly, when the team's explosive offense scored quickly and often. And a second half that prompted memories of recent ignominy—namely last season when Oregon finished 4-8 and had the worst defense in all of college football.

That last year's team actually won four games and came close in a couple of others was a testament to the talent level of the Ducks' young offensive players.

That talent was demonstrated again on Saturday—at least in the first half—and Oregon will have a chance again to win more than they lose.

But they need to play fast both halves, which they did not do against Nebraska. Kelly seldom slowed his teams down, unless he was nursing a lead in the fourth quarter, or didn't want to embarrass the other team.

Oregon played the second half to not lose—which is as old-fashioned as an offensive huddle.

Oregon's defense is only slightly better this year but has some nice new parts, with the addition of some beef up front and a couple of mega-talents in the secondary.

Oregon's "gonna have to score a ton," as ex-Oregon coach Mark Helfrich might say, because the defense is being rebuilt from the ground up.

I think you'll see more close games this year, and fewer blowouts like last year's Washington game at Autzen when the Huskies slapped 70 on a Duck team that quit, thus starting the countdown to a coaching change.

The Ducks have good-to-great talent scattered throughout their roster. They're looking for identity and cohesiveness and the next step forward.

Willie Taggart is the man now, and he's going to have his coaching chops tested in a very powerful league for the first time in his career.

We'll see how it goes.

FRIDAY, OCTOBER 3, 2014

New Cycle of Ugliness Coming

You knew they would, but man the boo birds are coming hard after Oregon today. A loss to Arizona will cause that.

No one—players, coaches, administrators, the ball boys—are exempt.

This is something I've never understood while being a long-time college football watcher in general and an Oregon fan specifically.

I started watching the Oregon program when I enrolled there in 1971. I've never missed a season, win or lose; the reason being I simply enjoy the game and the excitement of college ball. And believe me; in the old days there was plenty to get frustrated by as well as to celebrate. One thing I made sure of through the messes over the years is that I had fun watching the game.

Being a fan can be frustrating, but wrapping your entire identity around the game and your school's football program is dumb. Oregon lost the game last night.

The fans are making themselves miserable by giving the entire enterprise too much importance, treating it like life and death.

Oregon's program has obviously fallen off, another cycle has begun. What more can you say?

Oregon's recent success has bred a lot of unreasonable behavior among the team's faithful. Now everybody is a coach and, miraculously, a program director. The arrogance of the many has recalibrated--bounced the needle from "we're great" to a "we're-too-good-to-stand-for-this" fantasia.

The fire-the-staff movement is on, something I won't participate in because, frankly, I don't think any of this is important in the midst of what ought to be an entertainment. My goal now is to block out the noise.

That's becoming very difficult to do.

Unacknowledged this morning is a point of realism that the faux-coaches in Oregon's fan base simply are unwilling to embrace.

Arizona has a better team. Better players. Better coaches. Like many, I mourn the fall, but it was as inevitable as the Oregon rain and the cycle of the seasons..

Things are about to get as ugly as a muddy snowbank in the winter. Queue the Vivaldi.

Sigh...

WEDNESDAY, FEBRUARY 1, 2012

Oregon's Haul

Oregon's 2012 football recruits.

The list is notable in that three are from Oregon and four from Texas. A sprinkling of other states is represented besides California, which has long been Oregon's prime recruiting territory.

Oregon is truly in the national picture now. One of the Texas kids said he was impressed with Oregon's nationally ranked broadcast journalism school.

See, some of these kids have their priorities in order. All of them think about landing in the NFL one day, but the smart ones are realistic and know they have a real educational opportunity that they can take advantage of in case their initial dreams are shot down.

The Willie Lyles imbroglio didn't seem to harm this top 20 class, nor did the threat of Chip Kelly leaving for the NFL turn off the early commits.

In fact, Oregon's lone five-star blue chip recruit, Arik Armstead, said Kelly's humor and honesty during a home visit last week sold him on the program.

The football fan inside me goes into hibernation now. It'll revive in April when spring practice begins.

SUNDAY, NOVEMBER 16, 2014

Good Times

Big day yesterday, lots of good football.

Too bad Miami couldn't pull off the win against Florida State. The 'Noles need a loss in the worst way. Doesn't appear they'll get one, however.

The Alabama vs. Miss. St. game went about as I expected.

Here in the PAC the season is far from over. The South Division has parity, parity, parity. Arizona State's unexpected (if you believe the "experts") loss to Oregon State has created a chaotic stew of possibilities in the stretch run. Too many scenarios exist for my level of comprehension, but it appears UCLA has the upper hand if the Bruins win out.

If...it's a big question.

Oregon is now the lone PAC team to "control its own destiny" relative to the playoff. But after Colorado next week, a team the experts say Oregon ought to whip handily, look who is next.

That is correct. The suddenly competent Beavers of OSU. It's like I wrote at the beginning of the season. Mike Riley, much under the critics' thumbs this season, always has his team playing well at season's end.

It took the magic of Marcus Mariota and Josh Huff to quell the Beavers late in the Civil War last season.

The naivest of Oregon's fans, the armchair-would-be coaches, will tell you OSU shouldn't be in the game, much less win it.

That's not reality. OSU has the things Oregon's realistic fans (me and a few others) dread: a resurgent running game and a deadly QB when he has time to throw it.

Like I say, the season is far from over.

But I'll look ahead like everyone else for a moment.

If you're Oregon, you don't want any part of a USC loaded with five-star talent. At the start of the season I picked USC to win the conference championship.

Here's the kicker if you're a regular fan and not a Duck honk like I am. USC vs. Oregon, with a playoff on the line for Oregon, would be amazing television.

Better even than last night's OSU show.

THURSDAY, OCTOBER 10, 2013

Give Me Eight

What the big boys say, being Gemmell and Miller at ESPN.

They're pretty much together on all but one of their picks. Gemmell has WSU beating OSU in what should be a very entertaining pass fest. I'll go with WSU as well, just a hunch because the game is in Pullman.

Expert as they are, they both take Oregon. I take Oregon, and keep my fingers crossed.

An Oregon loss this weekend wouldn't be as crushing as last year's late-season OT loss to Stanford at Autzen—nothing is comparable to that in my experience, not even the loss to Auburn in the 2011 NC game.

At Washington this weekend a loss would hurt just a little bit, but I take Oregon by a TD. This season is young, with the tough games acomin.'

Is Oregon any good? Remember, they haven't played anybody.

Will the Lyerla fiasco count for anything?

Last year, after Stanford, I couldn't get out of bed for a week, so saddened was I by the blown opportunity. Oregon was ranked number 1 going into the game and poised for a shot at Notre Dame.

Oregon flat out wilted and Chip Kelly didn't help matters by constantly, stubbornly, maddeningly running plays to Stanford's strength—its D-line.

Oregon needed to attempt to pass more. Kelly went all conservative like Rick Santorum.

Woe is me... (Here I am coach-blaming.)

Notre Dame used its lucky charms to play in the championship game, the ridiculous result of a computerized system fueled by money and tradition and which hadn't anything at all to do with the relative strengths of the teams at the top of college football.

Welcome to this year's crappy system—same as it ever was—the last before a four team playoff commences next year, which btw is still a crock.

That is not solely because Condi Rice, that bright moron, may be involved.

Eight or bust.

Eight, I say.

THURSDAY, AUGUST 8, 2013

The Grind

I glanced at a couple of preseason pro football games this evening just for the hell of it, though I'm not a big pro football fan—I prefer the college game.

I'm not sure why this is to tell you the truth; though I think I simply prefer the college game's aesthetics. Despite making inroads recently, the NFL lacks the creativity of the college game. It is more brute strength and dominant speed. The game's best players tend to equalize each other on the field. The game becomes a grind. Explosion plays are rarer than they are in college, where explosion plays are a great part of the game and fun to watch.

I watched a little of the 49ers/Broncos game this evening. I liked the 49ers' LaMichael James when he starred at Oregon. In the pro game, he's just another player. He'll be fine and likely have a good, if short, career. But the explosiveness I'd come to unrealistically expect from James wasn't there tonight. Everybody on the field was as strong and fast as LaMichael James.

Once his first-team line exited the game, Denver's defense stopped him cold. That's the pro game. It can be as brutally boring as soccer.

The pro game likely isn't as corrupt as the college game because it doesn't have the NCAA in a corrupt leadership role. Businessmen run the pro game, and all you can make of it is what it is—a very expensive business venture that very rich elites promote as entertainment. With television deals and sellout crowds, they make a lot of money after paying out initially for players and ownership rights. They take a share of everything, including hot dog and beer sales in some places, I'm sure.

If the pro game is corrupt it is corrupt in a way completely different than the college game. The college game packs a more subtle form of corruption.

Pro players are well compensated, though their careers are short. A calculated honesty necessarily steers the game, I think. Everybody wins—until they lose. That's the nature of real, unfettered business.

Here is what happens to unfortunate former college players at the moment of truth—the moment they learn the future is uncertain and a big contract is unlikely.

One of the more fortunate ones, James signed a four-year deal for $10 million guaranteed.

Decent money, but it comes with risks people don't like to talk about. Like all players, professional or collegiate, he might lose his future good sense, as head injuries happen. Football, particularly pro ball, has a huge PR problem and even greater financial risks for the future. The game is dangerous, like mining and fighting fires. The social costs of football are being weighed for the first time by critics. People are striving to make the game safer.

The NCAA likes to pretend the game is more than a business. Sure, if select kids want to get an education while playing the game at one of the 120 big-time programs in the US they can honestly do that. It's up to them, though. The scholarship is a good deal for a kid who can snag one. The education, the very degree, promises nothing—for a football player who earns one for free or for a scholar who pays to play the education game.

The NCAA reaps billions in profits off the labor and risks its college football athletes take, and if the football idol the institution has created and used sells his autograph while still in school his career is potentially over.

Two equally abhorrent things are happening here. They are relative to one another only to the degree that capitalism allows them to be. The college player is being exploited like a low-wage earner at Wal-Mart. And regular college kids are getting ripped off by a system that forces them to pay too much for an education.

No, I shouldn't like big-time college football as much as I do.

OCTOBER 10, 2016

On the Edge

Unlike the majority of Oregon's loudest fans I still like Helfrich, despite his down season. I'd keep him around, mainly because I don't see another coach out there who would be a decent replacement.

The deal with coaches is most of them are meatheads. In the PAC-12 alone you have Jim Mora (huge ego, angry and under-performing), Sonny Dykes, who can't get it done at Cal, and the two Arizona schools' coaches, both vulgar meatheads who stomp around on the sidelines like apes; all have managed to have disastrous seasons just like Oregon's.

If Helfrich is fired, the program will fall even more than it has now. It'll take longer to come back, too.

Update: Oregon's AD, Rob Mullens, is bungling his job big time as of right now. Seems to be either a coward or immensely confused, likely a little of both.

Here's the thing. Some players signed on for next year because they like the staff that is there, despite the on-field struggles this season. Now several of the better recruits are looking elsewhere.

Oregon's unrealistic expectations remind me of national politics, wherein our crazed working men and women (or unemployed men and women) went ahead against all good sense and voted for Trump.

Mullens is kind of a Clinton-like figure, frozen like a deer in the headlights of an oncoming truck.

I've never liked Nike's influence on the team. For that matter I didn't like Chip Kelly as the head man at Oregon, but there's no arguing that he was innovative at the time and could motivate his players. He won a lot, and should have won a national championship in his second year.

Guys like Kelly (during his limited college run), Nick Saban and Urban Meyer of tOSU are pretty rare. The latter two were the right guys at two of the biggest football factories in the history of the game. They took those jobs because they knew they could win there more readily than elsewhere. Oregon isn't in that league, wasn't even with Kelly.

Everyone else in the discussion is marginal. Everybody has warts.

Here's something to think about. The Michigan State team that played in the BCS playoff last season fell to 4--8 this year.

People aren't clamoring for Mark Dantonio's head like Oregon's bandwagon fans are dogging Helfrich.

It's a sticky wicket, but this is one time when I think change is unnecessary and likely stupid over the long haul.

Well, everyone has an opinion, and there you have mine.

I wish Mullens had one, but like someone else wrote today—he's probably waiting for Phil Knight to tell him what to do.

MONDAY, OCTOBER 7, 2013

Colt vs. Oregon

Of late I haven't been wrong about much in my thinking. Sometimes I amaze myself. I'm really a lot brighter than Dooley gives me credit for. On Friday, I wrote this regarding Oregon's football team and what I see as its stellar team cohesion and mentality:

You never really know, because so much of it is hidden from public view, but it seems like Oregon has a great mentality this season, cohesiveness and team concept that is sterling. It's pretty clear that Oregon's style is to tell its kids that hard work is mandatory inside the program. If you can't do that, pack your bags. An interesting aspect of any program you follow is to watch the end of the season and see who disappears and ascertain why. Many kids don't like to sit on the bench in college after being stars in high school, so attrition plays into the game. Some simply decide college isn't for them.

We didn't have to wait for the end of the season, did we? Sunday, Colt Lyerla quit, packed his bags. One, he didn't abide by the Oregon credo of hard work all the time. Two, college was the wrong place for him.

This hurts the team for now, but it is best for the program going forward

THURSDAY, SEPTEMBER 4, 2014

The Real Big Game

The most intriguing college football game of the weekend is Oregon and Michigan State.

But most intriguing is not the same as most important.

While Saturday's Oregon vs. Michigan State game is getting most of the hype around the country, I think the Stanford vs. USC game is more important in the big picture, at least from the POV of PAC followers.

The big picture is the final four of the new College Football Playoff.

People are naturally curious about Oregon and whether the Ducks have the defense to play with the Spartans. They're also interested to see if Mariota can finally overcome a rugged, physical defense such as MSU's. He's healthy again, so perhaps he will.

Based on what I saw last weekend, however, I think Oregon is in trouble. Poor linebacker play cost the Ducks at the end of last season, and I expect that to continue because I just don't think they have the athletes at that position to compete at a high level.

Oregon will score, but not at its usual clip. The game will be tight, unless MSU simply road grades the Ducks, in which case it might turn ugly for the Eugene mob.

Stanford and USC is the more important game at this stage because it's a counter in conference. The winner has a leg up and USC avoids Oregon in a scheduling quirk.

Everybody is dangerous in the league, including WSU and OSU, so having that early conference lead is ultra-important.

FRIDAY, SEPTEMBER 20, 2013

Publishing: Santa and CD

Charles Deemer's new book of poetry, his fifth publication for RBP, is primed and ready for release, Oct. 26.

We selected this date to coincide with CD's 74th birthday (you're kidding me; only yesterday we were young and raising hell in Northwest Portland) and this season's big UCLA vs. Oregon football game, capping what the one-time Cal Tech quarterback imagines will be a crowning triptych of the mind—a celebration of survival, a humiliating loss to his Bruins by Nike University, and the appearance of the poems in *A Majority of One.*

Two for three ain't bad. I can't blame him for being sentimental, even delusional, but I hope he is not too disappointed when Oregon crushes UCLA that day.

While we both understand football to be an entertainment and convenient diversion, we also know that the publication of a good book takes precedence—in this case it also becomes a shield, a salve to the wounds CD will suffer when Oregon puts up 50 before halftime and his team calls it quits.

As we move closer to publishing—and the bloody battle—I'll post a few of the poems here and attempt to explain why I like them so much, along with my obnoxious analysis of what makes Oregon so darn good.

Meanwhile, I also have the photos and text for Lee Santa's jazz memoir, *A Journey into Jazz: Anecdotes, Notes and Photos of a Jazz Fan*, at hand.

I'm busy editing that. Look for it in January; a profound way to begin a new year, RBP's fourth in its remarkable quest to enrich your lives

TUESDAY, JANUARY 3, 2012

Not Bad, Just Not Good Enough

It feels a little anti-climactic now, the Ducks' victory in the Rose Bowl.

The Oregon football program has been good for so many seasons in a row that winning a meaningful game—that is becoming champion of something besides the PAC—was only a matter of time.

The Rose Bowl last night felt like just another game, which, interestingly, is exactly what Darron Thomas said in a post-game interview.

It hadn't sunk in for Thomas in other words that winning the Rose Bowl is a significant accomplishment. The game felt like any other to Thomas, who has lost just three games in two seasons as Oregon's starting quarterback.

Winning a lot in a sense makes one jaded, expectant of the desired results. Perhaps that is one way of measuring both the depth of my boredom at season's end and the stature of the Oregon program under the leadership of Chip Kelly.

Twenty years ago I might have been overwhelmed with excitement about what happened yesterday in Pasadena.

These days I prefer to rue last season when Oregon should have beaten Auburn in the national championship game.

(Always keeping that negativity close, because that's where one best controls it.)

The Rose Bowl is nice, if not the ultimate football prize. It'll be interesting to see how things play out next year, with Darron Thomas returning for a third season, with the stunningly gifted De'Anthony Thomas earning more carries in the likely absence of LaMichael James, and with 34 of 44 players returning from the two-deep roster, many of them young stars ready to shine.

Maybe I'll conjure interest in the championship game this week, but it's unlikely, because I really have no use for LSU and Alabama, despite knowing they are both excellent.

It feels to me like the season is finally over.

Good.

SUNDAY, JANUARY 3, 2016

Ugh...No Depth

That Oregon football game last night made a lot of people sick.

However, it merely made me queasy. I asked for excitement. I got that and a dose of disillusionment.

I've never seen anything quite like it, except that time in the early '90s at Cal when the Ducks blew a 33-0 halftime lead and lost.

But even that wasn't as ugly as this mess. It is as if Oregon took great care to lose. One false move and they could have shocked people and pulled off an upset.

Last night was a perfect storm of ineptitude across the board. You could see it coming from the moment a knocked-out Vernon Adams dropped like a dead body to the Alamodome turf. There was simply too much past evidence of the team's problems rearing up without the gifted EWU transfer.

The players quit. The defense grew tired. Even the coaches figured they couldn't win without VA, so they stopped coaching.

I haven't seen a team lose interest in the proceedings that fast since my own high school teams used to go out weekly and lose 60-0.

Oregon has issues, but I think they can be resolved and the team ought to bounce back next year.

Or maybe, despite my gloom, I'm just an optimist. Helfrich will probably seek out a new defensive coordinator. If he doesn't he'll be jeopardizing his own coaching future.

But really, it's a good thing this season is finally over. Everybody, including the team's harshest critics, would be wise to take a break.

There really is no need to get nasty. Save that shit for the politicians.

PAC basketball starts today when Oregon plays OSU at 4 p.m.

MONDAY, SEPTEMBER 3, 2012

The Weekend

The big story of the weekend was football-related. The season finally arrived.

I managed to escape the unbearable lightness of being this weekend while enjoying a couple of games that I had long looked forward to.

Life is eighty-percent dread and twenty-percent something else, one reason I like to be entertained. Quite incapable of entertaining myself, I rely on diversions to find contentment. To not do this is to invite madness, which is always near-at-hand anyway.

Like many football fans over the weekend I was curious about the quarterback situation at Oregon. I'd say they have a good one based on his short appearance Saturday night.

My experience back in the day dictated that the team's best athlete didn't usually win the quarterbacking job. The job went to the brightest fellow. His smarts didn't have to be what are now referred to as football smarts, but the other kind.

Book smarts. Football smarts didn't matter (they hadn't been invented).

He had to be a scholar in other words.

That policy had average kids like me confused. Why, I wondered, did Joe play quarterback when he was neither a good passer nor fast runner? It didn't make sense, and if the point wasn't to win why was I out there busting my ass?

My old team was regularly humiliated when I played in high school, and I always felt that happened in part because we had the wrong guy under center.

We didn't have a chance given that reality. The final score could have at least been closer.

I certainly didn't enjoy getting thumped every Friday night on the football field back then, just as I do not like being thumped at anything today.

Who does?

My quarterback, Joe, was student body president and a straight A scholar. He also had a great faith in God and threw up a lot of prayers that weren't answered.

He couldn't play football a lick. Naturally, I disliked him because Tom or Don should have been playing quarterback.

One notices injustice, or should.

MONDAY, JUNE 11, 2012

Ducks Lose to Kent State

Damn...Baseball can be a sudden charge, win or lose. I'm crushed, but I recall there is no crying in baseball.

No Omaha this year. I'll wait for football now.

SUNDAY, SEPTEMBER 4, 2011

The Big Game a Big Dud

There's no crying in football, but I feel like crying.

The Mighty Oregon Ducks fell hard last night to the mean old SEC again. It was close for a half, but Oregon didn't have the horses, finally, to stay with a fast, aggressive LSU team.

Darron Thomas looked ordinary, missing receivers too often. I said here earlier that Oregon needs to replace Jeff Maehl. No one showed that kind of ability for the Ducks last night as every one of the wideouts managed to drop a pass.

The returning wideouts, Huff and Tuinei, couldn't get separation from LSU's DBs, making it that much more difficult to pass successfully.

Thomas only occasionally threaded the needle. He's no Aaron Rodgers in that regard.

Worse, Oregon's bread and butter, its running game, were stale and moldy.

If any goodness comes out of this defeat it could be said that Oregon, while not a top 5 team, still has plenty to play for this year.

The Pac-12 will be more to their liking, though I suspect there will be a few nail biters throughout the season.

The Ducks are a very young team. Last night, it showed, translating into fumbles, bad penalties, and poor decision-making on many fronts.

Oregon must regroup for Nevada in friendly Autzen next week.

I'm saying they should win that one. But you never know.

MONDAY, AUGUST 12, 2013

Off Course

This story from the *Eugene Register Guard* has the hyper-kinetic fanboys on the football message boards all riled up.

Though I too love Oregon football, I just don't understand the intractable feelings some of its hardcore fans express whenever the program is justifiably criticized.

Clearly, many of them do not understand the role of the press in society (as an aside I'll point out that the press often abdicates its own role in society, but that is not the issue here). They honestly seem to believe that the function of the *Guard* ought to be to lead the cheers for the home town team. Rah, rah.

I believe the Football Psyops Center at Oregon is an embarrassment, as I've noted for the record.

Other than giving too much license to the one interviewee who couldn't express an idea without cloaking it in a deliberate cliché, and the reliance on a military man who attempts to smooth over the base nastiness of war (the mention of the sanctity of the Geneva Conventions in the context of America's recent wars, or modern warfare in general, is absurd), the article makes some good points.

Yeah sure, football would be better if it was run like the military. Given its sometimes mindlessness, I think they're already too close.

That is as offensive to me as the Psyops Center.

FRIDAY, AUGUST 24, 2012

A Fan's Notes

The college football world turns its collective gaze to Eugene today to find out who starts the season as Oregon's quarterback. The choice: Bryan Bennett or Marcus Mariota.

I personally think too much is made of decisions like the one head coach Chip Kelly will announce later this morning. One young man will be anointed the role of savior for this season; the other will take a clipboard to the sideline and keep notes.

Oregon is in the enviable position of having two fine young quarterbacks that could play just about anywhere except USC this year, where the incumbent golden boy, Matt Barkley, is said to walk on water.

But one of Oregon's guys is going to be very unhappy at the end of the day. Will a sudden transfer be the second headline soon thereafter?

The funny deal is that both Bennett and Mariota are likely to play a lot in the early season, unless Oregon is vastly overrated and finds itself struggling against teams it is supposed to handle with ease.

First up next Saturday is Arkansas State. ASU had a fine season last year, finishing 10-3, and has the core of that team returning and a new head coach with pedigree. Gus Malzahn coached at football hotbed Auburn and knows his stuff.

But the Sun Belt Conference is a mid-major conference and supposedly is unworthy of competing with the big boys of the PAC.

We'll see.

The day is drawing near, folks. If you've read this blog with the diligence that I have long suspected of you, you understand that college football is my number one entertainment.

Some folks prefer a long bike ride along a sunny path, but I'd rather sit at the bar or on my sofa and watch others exercise.

I like college football better than bad movies in the Cineplex; a carnival ride doesn't compare. Hiking and mountain climbing are not even close; a long walk on the beach with a fine babe is okay, as long as it winds up near a television by 9 a.m. PT on Saturday mornings when the weekly ritual begins.

If she sits down next to me in the bar and consumes the game with the same passion I have she will win my heart.

Hell, I'll buy her a beer if she wants one.

Next Saturday I shall celebrate the dawning of a vital new thing, an annual second lease on life, an otherworldly experience that some have compared to the ingestion of a good drug.

Is the quarterback drama playing out in Eugene today?

I don't care who gets the job as long as the Ducks win, baby. Yeah!

MONDAY, SEPTEMBER 9, 2013

Week Two

Notes on the football weekend past:

He has the best name in college football this year, but Munchie Legaux went down with a season-ending injury in Cincinnati's loss to Illinois.

Fortunately, he doesn't have to play to keep his best-name title because the other guy with a dazzling handle isn't playing either—Jadeveon Clowney is simply going through the motions while criticizing his coaches, two of whom appear to dislike each other.

Or is that just heat-of-battle stuff?

UCLA lost a player to a horrible accident unrelated to football Sunday morning. How will his teammates respond as they prepare for this weekend's big game with Nebraska?

UCLA and Washington had the weekend off; they're to be scrutinized closely this week because both appear to be legitimate threats to Stanford and Oregon dominance in Pac-12 play.

Ha! Ha! Ha! USC lost at home to Washington State and tumbled out of the Top 25. Ha! Ha! Ha!

I graded Oregon's new coaches up and down with equal vigor Saturday. Like the players, they were inconsistent. Mariota's QB draw was brilliantly conceived and executed, but...but...

Despite the trendy status quo Oregon popularized in college ball, which dictates a go go go offense all the time, the Ducks needed to slow things down and evaluate what was in front of them at times Saturday.

Virginia's defense was ready for the fast stuff. Oregon's uber-talent won that game but the offense hurried itself out of a couple of good first-half drives and at least one touchdown.

Am I sinning by saying so?

Three-and-out is not the Oregon way, and Dooley doesn't want to see it happen very often, citing a history of irritable bowel syndrome caused by stubborn, ineffective play-calling.

The looming question of the week—will Thomas Tyner play early in the game Saturday vs. Tennessee?

The kid appears to be slicker than the snot on a lunatic's nose, so give him a few carries in the first quarter and see what happens.

My heart-breaking, deeply unappreciated neighborhood Vikings—you had a chance. You did well, but came up just short.

I won't quit on you, though. I think you'll make a statement in the Big Sky this year. Portland is yours if you want her.

TUESDAY, JUNE 21, 2011

My Oregon Prophecy

The corruption at my university, sadly, appears to run into the murky depths.

I'm talking about the football program. In a post last season I reminded everybody that Nike University's program would one day crash to earth, the victim of a self-destructive scandal.

The day has arrived with the entanglement of Willie Lyles and Chip Kelly.

Given the current state of corruption in college sports (mainly football and basketball) my prophecy was a no-brainer, of course.

I just didn't think it would happen so soon after the program's back-to-back PAC-10 titles.

I don't see Chip Kelly surviving this. It looks incredibly dumb. I love college football and I wish it would (could) change, but it won't. Not with the billions involved.

I can tell you this much—college coaches in big-time football and basketball are drastically over-paid. That in itself leads to corruption.

The players? Let's face it; they're used and abused by the present system.

I'm laughing through my heartbreak.

SUNDAY, NOVEMBER 24, 2013

Corporate Football

There are observers who simply want Oregon to lose because Nike sponsors the school's athletic programs.

I would say one can't fight those sentiments—they are in fact self-evident and one can't be blamed for going there.

Much can be said for taking corporations out of college football, but it likely won't happen because FBS football is big business and, sorry as it is, corporations rule America.

There isn't a football program in the country, big or small, that hasn't some level of corporate sponsorship. Oregon State has the Reser family, the makers of bad potato salad. Oklahoma State has T. Boone Pickens, oilman.

Oregon had Thomas J. Autzen, a lumberman, before Mr. Knight.

I wish Nike would go away also, along with Condi Rice at Stanford. She ought to be on trial for complicity to commit genocide. In fact, of the Stanford grads, I favor Phil, who simply exploits Third World workers. He seems more benign, but barely.

Secretly, I want every privately endowed university in the land to go tits up because I'm tired of the class war.

Now, tell me George W. Bush got into Harvard and Yale on merit alone.

Heh, heh, heh...

WEDNESDAY, SEPTEMBER 25, 2013

Have another Hit

Four of the five Pac-12 games this weekend start at 7 p.m. (PT) or later. The Oregon State/Colorado game in Corvallis is the lone exception. That one kicks off at 3 p.m.

This is scheduling designed by TV network moguls, and it is unfortunate. The PAC is strong this year, but with this kind of coverage casual fans that live east of the Mississippi won't have a chance to gauge the conference for themselves.

Most of them will be counting sheep in their sleep rather than counting TDs when some of the PAC's best teams are racking up the points in the wee hours EDT.

Does it matter? Of course not, but allow me...

I long for the good old days when every game started at 1:00 local time. During my two years in Eugene while attending Oregon I went to every home game, didn't miss a single one. There was a pleasant symmetry to college-football Saturdays back then.

Get up, take a toke. Go to breakfast, take a toke. Go to the store and buy wine for the bota bag, take a toke. Walk the footbridge across the Willamette to Autzen, take a toke...

Sit in glorious sunshine (even if it rained) and watch football the way it was meant to be enjoyed (toked up).

Ah...

You could toke up in the stands back then, too. There weren't very many people at the games. Security was sort of lax, unlike today.

That paper due on Monday? I spewed it out on Sunday between tokes.

Most easterners will miss what ought to be a fantastic night in Seattle, where Washington State hosts Stanford at CenturyLink Field in a game I think WSU has a realistic chance of winning.

Or am I just high?

Across town, on the edge of Lake Washington, the Huskies host Arizona in a game featuring two of the nation's best running backs, Arizona's Ka'Deem Carey and Washington's Bishop Sankey, both of whom average nearly 150 YPG.

Talk about entertainment...with or without a toke.

Hardcore eastern football fans know about the PAC, but they're usually sleep deprived and so few in number that the sheer mass of the uninformed confirms the rule of ignorance—one of the disadvantages of democracy you could surmise.

Talking sense to the casual east coast fan about college ball is like trying to tell a teabagger convention about truth and justice. Hopeless.

Many of them had a little taste of Oregon earlier this month when the Ducks went out to Charlottesville and pounded Virginia.

It doesn't matter. Denial has always been big in the South.

Well, the Ducks weren't playing Florida State, Clemson or Alabama, so the PAC is irrelevant. Right?

They'll be a sorry lot if Cal comes into Autzen and upsets Oregon this weekend, won't they?

Not likely to happen, but if I lived back there and wanted somebody to beat the Ducks I'd be up all night, blurry-eyed, hoping against hope.

But then I'm a hardcore fan like my wasted, toked up brethren in Hoboken, who'll stay up all night to watch a real game.

FRIDAY, OCTOBER 1, 2010

Nike U.

Before it all comes crashing down--and it will crash back to Earth in a resounding explosion of corrupt venality—I plan to enjoy the football success of my university, the University of Oregon, AKA, Nike University. Why? Because it is an entertainment and a release from the dogged anguish of everyday life.

Hey, but it's the only television I watch!

To begin to understand college football today one must first accept the fact that it is big business (all of it, not just Oregon) meaning all its attendant problems of corruption are openly discernible. Those problems, however, are no more absolute or astonishing than the-just-as common corruption inherent in damn near every other American institution.

I don't like banks, but I have an account (for now). That in itself makes me a hypocrite.

I sometimes buy products that I don't actually need and which are harmful to my health (beer and cigs). But I don't buy Nike products, because they are ridiculously overpriced and, frankly, I think slapping logos on any wear other than team uniforms is a joke.

Nike didn't start that trend, by the way. When I played high school football I wore Puma cleats and MacGregor gear.

And I am all too aware that Nike manufactures in the Third World, costing American jobs and exploiting the peoples of other nations.

I spend money (fuck money) on poor and costly prefab food.

I am occasionally intellectually dishonest.

I am a football fan, but more a fan of the institution of higher learning (supposedly) where I met, years ago, some of the most unique individuals I've ever met. I knew it was corrupt when I enrolled.

I'm probably not as radical as I should be, but I believe Bush and Cheney should be jailed, Obama should be impeached, and the U.S. government should be brought to its knees to beg the forgiveness of millions of unemployed and underemployed workers and their children.

Saturday's final score: Oregon 42-38 in a doozy.

TUESDAY, JANUARY 17, 2017

Training?

Football boot camp started at the University of Oregon after the holiday break, and a few players are paying the price.

The coaches are playing a dangerous game with the health of their players.

This nonsense better be resolved quickly, better not happen again, or I'll be forced to do something I've never even considered before--that is call for a coaching change right now.

I've never made the call after a losing season, because I've always watched Oregon play regardless of their talent level year in and year out, and it doesn't matter too much to me how a season goes. Sure, I like to see the wins, but I don't go off the rails if the team loses and has a poor season like the one just finished.

But this is the sort of thing that pisses me off.

Football has enough militarism in it already without this kind of macho posing. Working players until they get sick is beyond the pale.

It's plain as day what happened. The three that ended up hospitalized were not in great shape coming in. Anybody who has ever exercised knows you can't get it back in a day, or even ten. You must build it up slowly until you return to peak levels.

More importantly, the coaches leading those exercises have to be alert to what condition the individual players are in. You can't herd them together and expect everybody to be on the same level, because that never happens. There are way too many variables in the process.

What happened? Under Willie Taggart and the new staff at Oregon the pressure is on to impress, indeed to keep schollies, to "do something." These players were feeling something they shouldn't have, and an escape route needed to be there for them without threatening their careers and educations. Some of the blame may be theirs, of course, but if the lax culture everybody is saying developed under Helfrich was problematic, what good is an adjustment to something plainly more dangerous?

Good lord, the game is dangerous enough as it is.

The strength coach is pushing people. Fine Sarg, but rein it in before somebody dies for a stupid game, not in a freakish play on the field but in your training facility where you supposedly have control of the proceedings.

I hope these players recover and can return to the team if they want to. If they don't want to, I would expect to hear the taunts of Oregon's worst fans, but as usual I say screw them.

UPDATE: Oregon has suspended the S&C coach and WT has apologized. Knuckleheads all over the internet are upset with the "pussies."

MONDAY, NOVEMBER 23, 2015

Don't Laugh, Cry

Don't laugh, but football is just like war. It really is, because Nike has designed cool camouflaged unis for Oregon's Civil War football game with OSU Friday afternoon.

You see, in the real world we're fighting wars to protect Nike and other major corporations from the Muslim rabble, the communists, and the union organizers in Third World manufacturing centers where workers are paid pennies on a dollar.

Which is how we like it right? How it should be?

So you and I can dress in Nike, mind you. So Oregon can win football games and look like warriors while doing it. Just doing it, I mean.

This is called "Freedom." All the boys and girls who would like to go to college or find a decent paying job are after all free to join the US Army and play out their football dreams on a battlefield of our government's choice.

There's plenty to choose from, too.

Everybody knows war is just like American football. Only, you know, more people die in an actual war.

OCTOBER 12, 2012

The Expert

I've been waiting, pondering, musing and otherwise trying to connect with my football instincts. I think I've settled on a kind of knowing, a certain confidence that I am a fully capable prognosticator.

I wanted to get a sense of the atmospheric conditions surrounding Oregon and Oregon State as they prepare for big games this weekend with UCLA and Stanford respectively.

This is Wednesday, ordinarily too early in the week to spill the beans, but I feel I know how these games will turn out. Like the weather outside, all is bright and embracing if you're an Oregonian with ties to either school.

Football fans in Oregon will be pleased. This weekend is going to be special, whether you are a die-hard Duck or a boastful Beaver.

I know a few Bruin fans who won't like what is going to happen Saturday. Despite my initial trepidation, I now believe Oregon will beat UCLA—perhaps not by the three TDs the touts in Vegas are predicting, but Oregon will win.

That is not perhaps a shocking pick—but here I pick up my game.

I think Mannion and Cooks will pass Stanford silly Saturday in Corvallis. Upset city.

In any case, I'm primed and ready for what should be a great day.

Now, if Tennessee could somehow knock off Alabama...

FRIDAY, DECEMBER 8, 2017

Football Report

Because big-time D-1 football has been reduced to a calculated political ploy to advance the agenda of the Power-5 conferences and make a ton of money for the usual suspects (ESPNSEC, etc.), and because you'd have to be a dolt like G.W. Bush to take seriously the CFP committee that has Condi Rice on board, and because a real playoff isn't coming to the FBS world any time soon...well, you don't have to despair.

The FCS 1-AA quarterfinals (the elite 8) commence tonight and continue tomorrow all day.

Just the excuse I need to avoid the Army/Navy game!

Speaking of football, Oregon promoted Mario Cristobal to its head coach position today, a hire I like personally because I think he's a better football coach than the one who left for Florida State.

You can tell he's a lot smarter than Taggart, if brains count for anything in college football, just by listening to him answer media questions.

Figures he's smart. He's an ex-Miami and NFL offensive lineman. O-linemen and QBs are usually the smartest players on any team.

Who knows? Maybe he'll stick around for a few years.

WEDNESDAY, NOVEMBER 22, 2017

To Hell with Duke

Some of college basketball's biggest stars, players and coaches, are headed to Portland for the PK80 this weekend, a basketball tournament to honor Nike founder Phil Knight a few weeks ahead of his 80th birthday.

Nike of course has revolutionized college sports on the backs of impoverished workers in Southeast Asia. The company has been doing so for years now.

Partnered with ESPN Events and the 16 Nike-branded schools involved, the world's largest sports-related apparel company is dressing everyone in fancy, colorful uniforms suitable for TV viewing and calling the Moda Center and the Memorial Coliseum home for three days of run and gun fun.

Like the hype around the modern game of basketball itself, the 16-team tourney (actually two simultaneous 8-team tournaments) at Portland's two large basketball arenas, is a bit of modern overkill.

Here is ESPN's description of the event Disney created to entertain basketball junkies and sell a shitload of advertising during this first of two traditional U.S. holidays; one being a gigantic celebration of gluttony and bird-slaughter while bestowing metaphysical thanks to our lucky stars that America's initial genocide turned out so well for the white man; the second being the annual shopping and gift-giving ritual that makes America great and theoretically devoted to Christ-like goodness, if not Christ himself.

In the West we shop to prove our faith in God and his celestial sun/son, while in other Kingdoms people tend to march off to sacred cities to show respect for the Great

Father, as happens in the Middle East during their sacred holidays.

Anyway, you can be sure that the poor laborers of Southeast Asia won't be in Portland this weekend to watch the game they've sewn their hearts out for, though some of their bosses surely will be. It's a spendy proposition.

But that's just the way it goes, doesn't it?

I'm debating whether I should spend my last centavos to go. I'm that fucking free, mind you, though as poor as a stitcher from "over there," the one with a travel ban tattooed on his forehead.

The tourney is just across the river and the concrete-jungle parking lot from my pad here in the good old USA, so at least I don't have to buy an airline ticket and rent a price-gouged hotel room for the weekend just to get a big boner on for my team, the Mighty Oregon Ducks.

On the football front, the annual game between Oregon and OSU, or the Civil War as it is quaintly known, will be played Saturday at 4 p.m.

Oregon must win to avoid a second straight embarrassing loss to the heavily dogged Beavs.

Oregon has its QB back. If he can stay on the field the Ducks should win—unless the unimaginable happens.

I don't want to think about it. Or, I'll put it this way. If first-year Oregon coach Willie Taggart really is contemplating jumping back to Florida next season because he misses the sunshine (which would be bad form), he'd best go ahead and leave if he loses to OSU.

Duck fans will otherwise make his life hellish.

FRIDAY, OCTOBER 30, 2015

Good Fun, Bad Vibes

Oregon beat ASU in an amazingly entertaining football game last night on ESPN.

Much of Oregon's fan base is in a bitching mood. The win wasn't good enough. That places Oregon in new territory for sure. I can't recall the last time, if ever, the Ducks started a season at 5-3 and had so many clamoring for a hatchet job on the program.

It's sad, not my cup of tea. I enjoyed the game and would gladly watch more like it. Well, in fact I do every Saturday throughout the college season.

Talk about misplaced priorities. The fans more so than the team are turning into a joke. The sense of entitlement is off the charts, a Nike-induced miasma.

When people can't accept change it makes for a lot of misery. The whole blame-it-on-the-coaches mentality that prevails right now is, frankly, stupid. Central to that is the misguided notion that Oregon's talent is superior to all others.

Reality doesn't suggest as much. The inability to understand that Oregon is not beyond the beyond is sort of funny—in a sad way.

SEPTEMBER 12, 2013

A Metaphor Too Far

This ought to be a Star Wars-style weekend of college ball. With both UCLA and Washington on furloughs last weekend, two of the PAC's best squads were MIA.

The MREs are a whole lot better this weekend, though Stanford vs. Army has the aura of an ugly "Highway of Death" mismatch and figures to be a real slaughter.

In other words, Stanford figures to drop a nuclear warhead on Army.

This is a game full of minefields for Army who will likely be KIA, if you know what I mean, like Custer.

I'm sorry, I don't mean to torture you (but if you have any complaints call Geneva, she'll know what to do).

I don't really care for Stanford's cerebral, CIA style, while admitting it is more effective than the SDI, obviously. The future EXXON executives took Oregon down last year at a most inopportune time by employing their Condoleezza Rice-designed, DOD-approved shock and awe strategy—that was Ed Reynolds chasing MM down from behind while DAT flaunted his ICBM-like speed at the front, thus missing the target and costing Oregon the battle, which lost the team a BCSNC medal—and thus the war.

Speaking of surveillance and more…

UCLA travels to Lincoln to play the Nebraska Cornhuskers in an intriguing Operation Groggy Morning conflict between ranked companies, and Washington takes a battalion across several rivers to Champaign, Illinois for night maneuvers a little later. These two skirmishes will provide us with some heretofore known unknowns about the strength of the PAC's insurgency across the USA.

I don't have enough listening and imaging devices to monitor all the action this weekend, and then there is this conflict of interest: Oregon and Tennessee trade sorties at the same time Alabama and TAMU get it on in the propaganda war of the week—it's Johnny Football vs. the Evil Empire.

If I surveille the action at home I can put up several windows at a time for maximum infiltration, I guess. Thanks to the miracle of computing technology passed down to us commoners by the MIC, I'll click back and forth like a drone pilot. But more likely I'll just grow immersed in the Oregon game and wait for the other games' highlights as I watch the carnage unfold from outer space.

Who doesn't like surveilling Oregon? Not me. I expect up-and-coming Tennessee to battle to the end like Davy Crockett. It ought to be entertaining as heck, unless the Ducks commit treason in the fourth quarter and expose their secret playbook as a sham.

If that happens I'll just kill myself and get it over with.

A case of PTSD. I won't LOL this time. I mean it.

FRIDAY, AUGUST 30, 2013

Nice Dog, Mean Man

Charles Deemer, whose new book of poems for RBP will come out in late October, is a mean-spirited anti-Duck.

That means while he was brave and smart enough to earn his MFA from Oregon, he hates the institution in Eugene, which he maliciously and habitually refers to as Nike U.

You know, because of Phil Knight's billion-dollar influence on athletics there.

In fact CD is a boisterous and illogical fan of UCLA, where he earned his undergraduate degree before attending Oregon, and not long after retiring as a Cold War military spy.

(Hmm...Was he a double agent?)

But now CD has gone beyond the pale. He is predicting that a major injury to one of Oregon's stars Saturday against Nicholls State University will change the lofty expectations for Oregon's season.

Call it Operation Crystal Ball, a Psyops maneuver by the enemy.

To even mention such a scenario is indicative of CD's calculating heart. To accomplish what he believes will happen, he expects the football gods to take down one of only two players who are so enormously valuable to the Ducks that an injury to either one would cause their dreams of glory to vanish.

In other words—and this is beyond dispute—our poet believes either Marcus Mariota or De'Anthony Thomas is going to suffer a season-ending injury in the first half of their game Saturday.

I don't know if Oregon will be unscathed after its first game, but I can tell you CD is playing dirty in this deadly game of prognostication.

THURSDAY, AUGUST 22, 2013

Getting Primed

I'm excited the college football season is almost here.

A week from today a handful of college teams kick off, including Portland State, which opens at home against Division III Eastern Oregon Thursday night. Not much to see there, but I might catch a little of it.

Speaking of mismatches, Oregon opens at home against Nicholls State next Saturday, a team that likely couldn't beat PSU. It would have been better for all concerned if PSU and Oregon had schemed to play each other in a friendly in-state to start the season. They've done that a couple of times in the past decade.

Oregon State also opens at home against a supposed lesser opponent in Eastern Washington, but EW plays at a higher level than either PSU or Nicholls State. I'll catch some of that one as well.

A couple of years ago, PSU played both Oregon and Arizona State and got crushed both times. They have Cal on Sept. 7; that is probably enough sacrifice for the big bucks in one year.

Saturday morning, I'll be ready to watch games from the Midwest and east coast. I watch all I can the first Saturday of every season.

After that, I discriminate a little more and pick a couple of games each weekend that sound appealing, while never passing on the Ducks.

THURSDAY, JANUARY 17, 2013

Chip to the NFL

Can Chip Kelly turn the Philadelphia Eagles around?

The L.A. Times' Chris DuFresnse says yes.

He says the NFL can use a shot in the arm given its stale conservatism and reliance on the status quo.

NFL analyst Heath Evans disagrees, calling Kelly's hire the "worst in NFL history."

Evans' words are hyperbolic given the NFL's often dull history. I mean there is a lot of competitive ineptness out there from over the years.

What do I think? Two answers: I don't know and it depends. One thing I do know, however, is that Evans' article is filled with factual errors regarding the Oregon program, which he obviously hasn't seen up close.

His argument that Oregon has the advantage of recruiting the "best" players in the land is mistaken. Oregon, under Mike Bellotti and Kelly, has never recruited a top-ten class.

That honor goes annually to Alabama, Notre Dame, USC and several other programs.

Oregon, in fact, has never had a consensus PAC "best class" of recruits. That distinction nearly always goes to USC.

Not coincidentally, Stanford's recruiting classes of the past five years have been better than Oregon's. It is no accident that Stanford finally had the players to defeat the Ducks this season.

What Kelly and Bellotti before him excelled at is coaching. They took middling athletes, with few exceptions, and coached them up.

Kelly's system, particularly, thrived on speed, which is only one advantage in the development of a football program. Others are size, quickness, technique, attitude, smarts, work ethic, etc., etc.

Will Kelly succeed? I don't know. I do know that he will make the professional game a little more interesting for those of us who find it to be somewhat stale and generally way too conservative.

Don't think for a moment that Pete Carroll in Seattle and Jim Harbaugh in San Francisco weren't paying attention during their PAC coaching years when Kelly's teams regularly beat them.

They have integrated elements of Kelly's method into their pro systems with positive results.

MONDAY, DECEMBER 3, 2012

The Dead Season

Would things work the way they should, big-time college football might be getting interesting now rather than wending down in its customary, bowl-infused, painful manner.

Eight teams would be seeded in a playoff format to determine which "institution of higher learning" in the land actually has the best football team, not that it matters one iota.

Don't get me wrong, I recognize that bowls are cool. The Kraft Hunger Bowl is cool, for instance, if you buy and ingest processed cheese.

I guess if you're hungry enough you'll watch anything.

The point is if they are going to play the games, the games ought to have a semblance of meaning, as they supposedly did all season long when teams battled to win their conference championships.

The format would resemble what the lower-division NCAA football schools do to determine their champions; that is they seed x-number of teams and go at it.

Major-college basketball does this, albeit to excess, and the post-season flourishes. A true champion emerges, no argument.

One day an eight-team college football playoff format will happen. It won't be perfect, but it'll beat what college fans must endure now while listening to the football pundits extol Notre Dame vs. Alabama.

I don't think either one could beat Oregon, or Stanford a second time.

But I have a west coast bias.

What am I getting out of the current BCS system except a month of boredom, the rumor of a championship, and the opportunity this weekend to watch Navy kick Army's ass?

Not much.

SATURDAY, APRIL 7, 2012

Glory Days

With spring football practice in full swing at Oregon and Oregon State, it's time to relive the glory of the 2012 Rose Bowl, wherein Nike U. beat Wisconsin in a thriller.

OSU unfortunately did not play well enough last season to go bowling, but they'll bounce back soon, I believe.

Oregon has lost a few stars from the Rose Bowl champs, but of late they've been able to reload at key positions—so perhaps Darron Thomas and LaMichael James will not be missed too much.

The most interesting aspect of the competition battle in Eugene this spring is at quarterback, where two kids vie to become the next big thing: Sophomore Bryan Bennett, who played a little last season, and redshirt Freshman Marcus Mariota, a big kid with a big arm who hasn't been on the field yet as a Duck.

I'll give the edge to Bennett. A little experience helps.

Both of these guys can run as well as throw it, something Darron Thomas couldn't do last year. Thomas was a leader, a sharp kid who knew the intricacies of the spread Oregon thrives on, but he wasn't very fast and had an erratic arm at times.

In coach speak; reps will bring the new QBs up to speed.

Oregon has a light opening schedule; I expect the QB situation to settle nicely by the time the PAC schedule begins in week four.

WEDNESDAY, DECEMBER 14, 2011

Moving On

This wasn't unexpected news, but it is still somewhat disappointing for a diehard Oregon fan like me. LaMichael James will move on after the Rose Bowl Jan. 2.

He'll sign a $2 million NFL contract and try to survive for three or four years in professional football, the average length of a running back's career in that violent world.

Good for him. The money will come in handy over the next fifty or sixty years.

James has been a good student and a fine representative of the university. A squabble with an ex-girlfriend got him in hot water before his sophomore season, but he's been standup ever since.

James broke into the Oregon lineup his redshirt-freshman year when LeGarrette Blount punched out a Boise State player and earned a season-long suspension for his trouble.

He didn't look back, leading Oregon to the 2009 Rose Bowl.

Last season, he carried Oregon all the way to the BCS National Championship game, rushing for over 1,700 yards and finishing third in the Heisman Trophy race.

This season, he rushed for over 200 yards four times and finished with 1,600 yards, despite missing two games with an arm injury.

His critics say he doesn't perform well against big, fast defenses, as happened against Ohio State and LSU in two of his biggest tests. My question is who does?

All James will need as a pro is a solid offensive line, because if he has an opening he's all speed. Yet, he's tougher than he looks.

LaMichael James is the greatest running back to ever play at Oregon.

He will be missed.

SUNDAY, NOVEMBER 20, 2011

How to Lose a Football Game

That truly would have been a miracle comeback.

After lollygagging around for most of the game and getting their butts kicked, the Ducks caught fire behind a couple of dumb USC miscues and nearly tied the game as the clock ran out last night in Eugene.

Oregon's mind wasn't on this game until it was too late.

When is a 37-yard field-goal not routine? When a possible National Championship is on the line, apparently.

This game had all the earmarks of a brewing disaster earlier in the week, when the media started yapping about Oregon's NCG chances.

The big win over Stanford last week lingered too long and became a distraction for the Ducks.

Players heard how great they are and lost focus.

Phil Knight invited a crowd of idle, bored NBA players to stand along the sidelines and they became a sideshow that diminished the intensity Oregon needed to compete with a highly skilled opponent.

Oregon wasn't ready. Maybe they learned something about handling the spotlight, maybe not.

Oregon State's chances in the Civil War just up-ticked.

Will LeBron and Dwayne be there for the Ducks on Saturday? Of course not. Last night's game was about Nike marketing, Phil Knight, and the star power of USC.

Chip Kelly should have told Phil no when the NBA circus landed. But then he would have likely been fired for insubordination.

MONDAY, NOVEMBER 15, 2010

The Toughest Test

Maybe it wasn't such a good idea to hammer the opposition week in and week out like Oregon had until Saturday's close victory over the Cal Bears.

Now people are calling the Ducks frauds, lucky, overrated, blah, blah, and blah.

Perhaps Oregon should have taken the foot off the pedal at certain times—you know, beat UCLA by fifteen and not thirty or more. They should have handled Washington with kid gloves, rather than clobber them with a rolling pin.

They could have let Stanford stay a little closer in the fourth quarter, win on a last second drive rather than going away.

The expectations of people, many of whom don't really understand the nuances of the game (some have played it, others haven't), create an unrealistic picture of what is involved in attempting to remain undefeated throughout a season.

Look at the top four teams in the current BCS standings. Among them, Boise State is the only team to not have a close call while remaining undefeated. But Boise doesn't play top-flight competition all year long. They beat a Virginia Tech team that managed to lose to James Madison the following week. By the way, JM plays second-level football, like Portland State.

Boise State also beat Oregon State. Well, a lot of luster has fallen off that win, considering that Washington State also beat the Beavers Saturday.

Boise doesn't have a quality win or a close game, in other words. They're good, but not that good.

TCU let San Diego State stay close until the end Saturday—the Horned Frogs won by five. Auburn has had four close calls this season, including three 3 point games. That's a field goal in each game, friends. But Auburn is great because they play in the supposedly regal SEC. Well one of those close calls was at Kentucky.

Kentucky?

Oregon has its Cal experience—a close call.

I'm not worried about Oregon's effort moving ahead. The players have that part of the game figured out. They know everybody is giving them their best shot.

Whether they beat Arizona by one point or fifty points on Nov. 26th doesn't concern me. They're at home and have something to prove, so I think they'll be fine, clinch the PAC title, guaranteeing a second consecutive Rose Bowl.

The Sears Cup is sitting in a vault in Glendale, Arizona. The Ducks want it bad—the Rose Bowl be damned.

But I think OSU in the league finale at Corvallis will be the Ducks' truest test. That final hurdle is always the highest one at the end of any race.

I didn't run track, but even I know that.

WEDNESDAY, NOVEMBER 29, 2017

Willie Taggart's Bad Form

Oregon offered Coach Willie Taggart a new deal last weekend with the hope that he'll stay in Eugene even if a coveted job in his home state opens this weekend, SI.com has learned. If Taggart accepts, the new deal would pay a little more than $20 million over five years. But Taggart has reason to wait. If Jimbo Fisher leaves Florida State for Texas A&M, Taggart could be a candidate for the Seminoles' job.—SI.com

Here in Oregon we're watching the slime ooze out of the beautiful game of American college football.

I wasn't a fan of this hire in the first place, figuring something like this would happen. You bring a guy in from Florida. He gets homesick and misses his recently widowed mother.

He talks a big game, raises platitudes to new heights. *Oregon is a great job, unlimited potential to win it all. Got everything, facilities, great fans, money up the yang hole, etc., etc.*

But in the end it is as meaningless as empty words.

I agree with this.

Oregon ought to be looking for a way to fire Willie Taggart and find someone who wants to be in Eugene—someone who will say it loud and clear and mean it.

No half-assed jokers. No con men. The game Taggart is playing is all about the bad form, the sleaze that surrounds college football and other games as well.

I'm tired of it.

FRIDAY, OCTOBER 27, 2017

Weekend Notes

…I could never vote for a Democrat who glorifies the military and its generals, and who pretends that our vaunted "troops" are "serving their country" and defending its freedoms when, in fact, they are serving an empire the very existence of which threatens the basic rights and liberties of all Americans

On the other hand, I would happily support anyone who would forthrightly state the obvious: that, with few exceptions, generals are mostly 'mad dogs" who like to kill or sleaze balls of the John F. Kelly variety; that soldiers are mostly economic conscripts; and that the last and perhaps the only time that the American military fired shots in defense of freedom was some seven decades ago, in the European theater of World War II.—AL

Start your weekend off the right way—er, left way, with the righteousness of Andrew Levine (*CounterPunch*, Oct. 27, 2017).

***

Damn, the Oregon State Beavers blew it last night and unfortunately avoided gifting college football watchers the best upset of the year.

How? The Beavers fumbled late in their own territory against Stanford, on a drive that would have iced the upset and made them instantaneous heroes to underdogs everywhere.

Ooh, that was sad to see. And wow, amazing how the Beavers have improved since their old coach quit at mid-season. There's suddenly hope in Corvallis...

Now OSU will have to seriously consider giving the job to the young, black former assistant who is interim coach and has the Beavers competing.

What, a black head coach at Oregon State? Hell I'm old enough to remember when OSU spurned blacks and a fat-headed racist named Dee Andros ran the show. They called him the "Great Pumpkin"—because the school's colors are orange and black and the coach, with his great belly covered by an orange jacket, sort of resembled a scary carved-out pumpkin. However, he was in my mind a bumpkin.

Seriously, something about the guy bugged me, though at the time I couldn't have put my finger on exactly what it was. I had an opportunity to "walk-on" and play for him, but didn't take it. One, I knew I was too slow and undersized to play major college football. But I didn't like Andros as well.

Oregon hired its first African-American coach this year in Willie Taggart, but I think OSU's guy, Cory Hall, might be a better coach and leader.

If OSU beats Oregon in the Civil War, the interim coach might get the job. Cool.

THURSDAY, JANUARY 8, 2015

One Year Later

What a difference a year makes.

This is what I wrote December 30, 2013 on the eve of the Alamo Bowl, which Oregon would go on to win while capping a two-loss season that disappointed many delusional Oregon fans.

As many fans petitioned to get rid of first-year coach Mark Helfrich and his able assistants, I grew depressed. So much nonsense, stupidity and self-righteousness made me angry and I wanted to give up on the college game.

Not because I had lost interest in the game, but because ignorance disappoints me. Obstinate and irrational people disappoint me.

Now Oregon sits ready to play Ohio State in the first-ever College Football Playoff, and the town criers have disappeared.

Thank the football gods for small favors—for now.

I have no idea who will win Monday night as the game and Oregon's season finishes up in Arlington, Texas.

But what a great pleasure it is to not be suffering the loud crowd of armchair experts bashing Helfrich's team at this moment.

TUESDAY, OCTOBER 15, 2013

Rumor Central

A rumor is circulating on the football boards that Oregon will don pink helmets this weekend in recognition of breast cancer awareness month.

I was hoping it would not come to this.

Gonna be ugly if it is true. I have the same reaction to the ubiquitous football pink you see everywhere this time of year that I have to the blue field at Boise State. I get sick looking at the colors, literally. I'm not kidding, they make me nauseous.

Besides, it is wrong, wrong, and wrong for other reasons.

I'm all for fighting cancer, but turning football into a mass-mind charity like the NFL has, wherein it keeps too much of the profits from selling the pink anti-cancer merchandise, is just another business ruse, a play on the sentimental in US society, like a fly-over of jet fighters before a bowl game.

Besides, being fashion conscious as I am, I know pink clashes with Oregon green—I will get sick if this happens. For me, the colors that usually dominate college football are part of the game's charm; pink will annihilate that.

This is an unnecessary distraction for the team and fans like me who deplore pink. If you must make this show of communion with the annual fundraiser, be tasteful for gawd's sake.

Wear a pink ribbon on your chest and call it a day.

This whole deal is, in short, idiotic. But this is America.

***

Mike Vick made a telling comment post-game last night, one I'd be worried about if I was a die-hard Eagles and Chip Kelly fan, which I'm not despite the coach's many victories at Oregon.

Vick told reporters that after the first quarter he felt like the Eagles had already played a half. He said, "It's going to be a long season."

In truth, Vick made the statements in a celebratory moment, but they have a double meaning. The fast-paced style, if it persists game after game, will wear the Eagles out.

Pro teams carry a roster of 53 players and play 16 grueling regular season games. The Eagles are back at it next Sunday, a scant six days from now. Will they recover in time from this first flourish of brutal, up-tempo exercise?

My theory is they'll be fine, even good, for a few weeks early in the season, but down the road they'll lose their legs. Vick is an old man by football standards, at 33. The kids will have a better chance of surviving for a longer period of time, but Vick is gonna be toasted soon enough.

If he holds up the entire season I'll buy you a beer.

The irony is I love this kind of football; it is one of the reasons I enjoy the college game more than the staid professional variety. But NCAA rosters have the numbers to play fast. Look at Oregon. Kelly's success there was predicated on having a lot of players. Thirty defensive players got in the game against Virginia last weekend. Most of them were Kelly's guys, players selected and molded to fit his approach to the game.

But in order for this to ultimately work league-wide in the NFL, teams will have to restructure their employment philosophies, pay the bucks to expand their rosters, and go for it.

They have no real incentive to do this, however. Pro football fans are among the most loyal in sports. Even losing teams sell out weekly, so why would owners want to change the scheme of things?

I look for the Eagles to go strong for half the season before fading into a tired-assed funk.

It'll be entertaining as hell for a while, but then it will settle into the ordinary show of typical professional football.

Slow down here, fellas. What's the hurry? We're makin' money, ain't we?

TUESDAY, FEBRUARY 19, 2013

Active Reading

The Richard Ben Cramer bio of Joe DiMaggio, a quirky book written in a kind of pseudo-illiterate vernacular that I guess is meant to reflect idioms of pre and post-WWII baseball life. I picked this up because the author died a couple of months ago and I figured it was time I paid my respect.

And it is nearly baseball season again.

As I worked my way through the first half of *Joe DiMaggio: The Hero's Life*, I paused to take on Robert B. Parker's last novel, *Sixkill*. A very thin plot driven by the late detective novelist's usual array of tricks and treats.

Sixkill is a Native American ex-football star who had a lesser game against Oregon in his final season before washing out behind booze and broads.

It was nice to see Parker's nod to the Oregon football franchise.

What a life I'm living, huh? Here I am working on little projects, buying time until my retirement kicks in next month, trying to stay sane amid the hue and cry.

I wouldn't have it any other way.

:

MONDAY, AUGUST 6, 2012

Riskin' Multitudinous Corruption

How many of y'all know what today is?

Probably not many of ya because y'all so bright and being literary types you could give a shit 'bout what I think, but I'll tell y'all anyways.

This is the first day of college football practice for the University of Oregon leadin' up to the Ducks' openin' game Sept. 1 against Arkansas State.

If y'all don't know what that means for this old country boy y'all ain't been payin' attention.

It means one, I'm back in the saddle and I'm as pleased as a pig in a slop farm.

It means two, I can start bitchin' about the way Chip Kelly has closed off his practice sessions at my alma mater and turned the public university's football program into a goddamn elitist secret affair that stinks just like that slop farm I'm talkin' 'bout.

Now let me be the third or fourth hundred folk to say it and say it nice 'n' loud.

By takin' the transparency out of that football program y'all be treadin' on some dangerous terrain.

Now I ain't sayin' the football program at the University of Oregon is approachin' Penn State's degree of multitudinous corruption.

I'm just' askin' why y'all even want to risk bein' so dumb?

And another thing folks. I'm really sorry 'bout slippin' into this phony country vernacular I been usin' in this post, but y'all see I been listenin' to so damn many country tunes of late, well, I'm startin' to talk like Tom T. Hall as I wait for the game with Arkie State.

MONDAY, NOVEMBER 28, 2011

History?

This is one of the strangest things I've ever heard of or witnessed in a lifetime of watching sporting events.

Rick Neuheisel, whose UCLA team plays Oregon in the inaugural Pac-12 football championship game on Friday night, has been fired after four years at the Westwood university.

He will be allowed to coach against Oregon, but no more.

His team has a .500 record and landed in the championship game after a fluke combination of events forced a tiebreaker among the also-rans of a PAC South Division dominated by the probation-stuck USC Trojans.

The Trojans demonstrated their skills in a victory over Oregon in Eugene two weeks ago. But they are ineligible to play for the PAC-12 title after getting nabbed two years ago for violating NCAA rules.

(The NCAA is a monolith of absurdity, but that is another story for another day.)

Yet, if UCLA manages to upset Oregon and go to the Rose Bowl, Neuheisel will not be coaching along the Bruins' sideline.

When is the last time a Rose Bowl-bound team fired its head coach on the eve of one of college football's grand showcases?

It has never happened. If UCLA were to upset Nike U. and get into the Rose Bowl, the strangeness of this 2011 season will be sealed for eternity.

SATURDAY, AUGUST 29, 2015

Depth Charges

Oregon's idiot bandwagon fans and uninformed loudmouths are already bitching about the coaching decisions that have left their favorite players off the "two-deep" lineup for Saturday's game against Eastern Washington.

The only seeming consensus is that, based on his career in FCS football and Jeff Lockie's inexperience, all Oregon fans seem to think the choice of Vernon Adams as the starting QB is a good thing.

Oh, and everybody is convinced Royce Freeman is the "real deal." Heh...

That one wasn't too tough.

Whoop-tee-doo.

The two-deep roster, no matter your team, is essentially the coaches' determination of which 44 players can best help the team win a game on any given Saturday. It is not chiseled in stone. Year-long, it is always a fluid thing dependent on the health and performance of each member of the team. It is highly mutable, under flux, and beyond any set notions of the "way things ought to be" as voiced by halfwits.

We're a week out from the start of the Oregon season, and the stupidity of Oregon's loudest, most obnoxious fan base is already getting on my nerves.

What's new?

How will I survive the season, especially if the Ducks happen to lose a game that the "experts" on the fan sites I read deem "unacceptable" and begin to spew negativity about the coaches and team?

I suppose I shouldn't indulge myself. I'll watch the games and try to tune out the hype, pro and con.

FRIDAY, OCTOBER 31, 2014

How does it feel...?

If you know me, you know I'm a college football junkie. If you know this you also likely know that the college game upsets me on occasion.

I mention as much here often enough.

You shouldn't care about that, of course, and I hope you don't. It's my problem after all, one I created for myself when I fell in love with the game as a youngster.

I never grew out of college football like I did, say, baseball or my eighth-grade blue jeans.

I like to watch college football. Years ago, I loved playing it during a single season in Ashland, Oregon.

These days a lot of crap surrounds the college game, most of it generated by the big money that has taken over the collegiality of the game.

For me, the aesthetics of the game are being pushed aside by the cash flow coming down from the mountain top—which here is a metaphor for television.

An article from *Rolling Stone* published a few days ago that succinctly sums up today's game and the problems generated by the enormous amount of money now attached to it (rollingstone.com, Oct. 28, 2014).

Worth a read, I say. You might like it because the author's first and last premise is the same; that football doesn't mean shit, but that the corruption now surrounding the game means everything.

THURSDAY, JANUARY 3, 2013

The Best

Somebody should throw an unsportsmanlike-conduct flag on RBP contributor Charles Deemer later today during the Fiesta Bowl.

He, along with a majority of other old-fashioned football pundits, doesn't like Oregon's Nike-made unis.

Throw the flag while he tailgates with a plateful of scrapple and black-eyed peas—and God knows what kind of insane and distasteful Starbucks concoction to wash it down with in front of his TV as he berates my favorite college football team for its supposed bad taste in apparel.

He should be reminded that beauty is in the eye of the beholder—in the culinary as well as the football arts.

That's fifteen yards and no dessert for you, CD.

FRIDAY, OCTOBER 19, 2012

Game Report

They weren't who I thought they were...

Arizona State University, that is.

I went out to a sports bar to watch last night's Oregon game. First time I've done that this season, I usually sit at home alone in front of my computer and stream the games, privately fretting and cringing as Marcus Mariota inexplicably drops the football on occasion and otherwise looks like he's in over his head.

But the kid repeatedly snaps out of it and makes plays, as he did last night.

The young Oregon QB had a good reason to drop one last night when Will Sutton charged untouched from the middle of the ASU line and smacked him upside the head. Sutton unfortunately hurt himself in the process and that was the ball game.

Without one of the country's best college linemen, ASU's defense fell apart and Oregon's dominate team speed expressed itself, running faster than a spoken disclaimer in a drug advertisement.

On the Ducks' second series, Kenjon Barner made a nice jump-cut at the line of scrimmage and ran through the space normally occupied by Sutton.

Seventy-yards later it was, See ya!

ASU wasn't who I thought they were, but Oregon's back-loaded PAC schedule gets tougher after next weekend's home date with Colorado.

Road games at USC, Cal and OSU loom.

I'll likely be at home once again afrettin' and asweatin' them out.

TUESDAY, OCTOBER 16, 2012

Eating the Young

There is a truism regarding college football that has me concerned about how Oregon might weather its Thursday night game at Tempe against a more veteran ASU team, as well as Oregon's campaign for a fourth straight PAC title.

Young players are prone to hit a wall at some point in the long season, particularly true freshmen. Their adaptation and acclimation to the rigors of the college regimen is crucial, as fatigue begins to settle in.

True freshmen are particularly vulnerable, which is why coaches would rather redshirt a frosh if possible.

Oregon is playing a lot of true freshmen now, relying on them in fact, due to some off-field issues and injuries. In the near future this will help them; right now it is a dangerous scenario.

Young minds begin to wander (some of us old guys' minds do as well), and the Zen-like focus that is required to maintain a top-notch performance level is prone to compromise.

Adjustments to the school schedule, the pressure of expectations, the new girlfriend, the growing yet immature body—all of these things factor into the performance of youngsters.

We'll see, but I won't be shocked if Oregon loses Thursday night. Tempe is tough in 90 degree heat against a solid veteran team, and in front of 70K hostile fans.

SUNDAY, OCTOBER 20, 2013

Hitting the Trifecta

The week ahead figures to be one of the biggest mankind have ever known.

Foremost among events, Charles Deemer's new book of poems, *A Majority of One*, will appear Saturday, which also happens to be the Round Bend Press stalwart's 74th birthday.

Deemer's latest, his fifth book for RBP, is filled with mirthful and wry observations on the human condition, which is Deemer at his best, whether he is contemplating his relationship with his dog Sketch or his own mortality as he prepares to retire from a long career in academia.

Throw in his usual salty observations regarding the body politic, and you have classic Deemer.

Lately CD has taken up the ukulele and wonders whether this new book will be his last "serious" work (as opposed to his Overdrive series of "entertainments"). A breath later he is conjuring up the plot of a new novel, a sequel to *Sodom, Gomorrah & Jones.*

With Deemer real retirement is merely an imagined thing, I think.

Not coincidentally, his football team plays my football team on Saturday as well. Deemer was a UCLA grad before earning his MFA at Oregon. I was an Oregon grad before earning my history degree at Portland State, where the poet teaches screenwriting.

O what a tangled web of intrigue Saturday will bring when UCLA plays Oregon in Eugene at 4 p.m.

We know the book is good and that Deemer is an old fart, but what will the day on the gridiron reveal?

WEDNESDAY, JANUARY 16, 2013

Keep Moving

It is about time Chip Kelly made up his mind.

A personality cult had seized the football program at Oregon, and that was not a good thing.

Despots and control freaks are a drag.

I was never a big fan of Chip Kelly, though I admired his results. His players seemed to love him by most accounts, so what I think doesn't matter.

I get the whole "that is a silly question" shtick that was his calling card while dealing with the media, but some tact in places would have been admirable in itself.

I lack that at times myself. We all do.

Kelly goes out a winner, but sanctions await the university's football program thanks to one of the dumbest moves an Oregon coach has ever made.

Paying Willie Lyles *beaucoup* bucks for nothing was absolutely as dumb as the media.

WEDNESDAY, APRIL 18, 2012

At Oregon: Smoke Weed and Win

Isn't it interesting that at Oregon some of the players claim 40 to 60 percent of the team smokes marijuana?

There are more potheads in the sports world now then there were 40 years ago, when I played football for one season at Southern Oregon College. But even back then players smoked, just like their hippie classmates.

Talk about culturally induced lifestyles. Of the four black players on the SOC team that year three of them smoked. The other one didn't feel like putting his commercial piloting dreams at risk and abstained.

Irwin (the pilot) was a great guy, but the other three were funnier, particularly when I indulged with them. Marvin was the funniest, a tall wide-receiver with pitch-fork hands who speared the ball out of the sky.

I prefer my pilots be tested and my football players be left alone with their pot.

I played baseball at an Oregon junior college the following year. Amphetamine was the go-to drug of choice on that team. I always figured that was because baseball can be sleep-inducing; speed keeps you awake, and ready to field that liner flashing towards your forehead if you play third, as I did.

The chief difference between then and now, I'd guess, without having any evidence of it, is that speed has probably lost favor among athletes, while pot consumption has likely grown along with its general use throughout American society.

Amphetamine is still the drug of choice among violent criminals, however, along with booze.

Pot prohibition is one of those silly laws that rankle for its lack of common sense. Alcohol is far more damaging to the liver and the soul.

Believe me, I should know.

I would argue that driving under the influence of anything is bad, particularly NASCAR. There are enough naturally stoned, redneck drivers out there already, along with a vast segment of people whose licenses should be revoked because they can't park.

In fact, I'm not much of a pot smoker now, nor have I ever been. I've socialized with it in ways that I haven't with booze; that is in a more earthy fashion. Drinking can easily become compulsive and addictive. Look around.

When I go on a drinking jag, bad things tend to happen. Nothing violent happens usually, but one's motor reflexes and good sense diminish rapidly, unless one is Irish.

Weed has never overwhelmed my good sense like booze has on many occasions.

I laughed reading an ESPN article (espn.com April 19, 2012) wherein a player noted—and I've heard this many, many times—"I don't even like beer, so I don't drink it." He had those loathsome munchies when he confessed this.

In order of their wasteful effects on humans, I say booze is number one, television is number two, and consumerism is number three. Stupidity ranks fourth. Or, arguably, number 1-A.

Pot is way down the list of my concerns, believe me, but try telling that to a politician who seeks the Christian voting bloc in an upcoming election.

We're a nation of hypocrites, no doubt about it.

THURSDAY, SEPTEMBER 1, 2011

Read All About It!

Led by the hardest working football writer in Oregon, Rob Moseley, the *Eugene Register-Guard* does a stellar job of covering my football team, the Mighty Oregon Ducks.

The Oregonian, with twice the number of beat writers covering the Ducks, simply can't compete with the RG's lock down coverage.

With kickoff of the UO vs. LSU top-five match up just two days away, the RG today published its fully-focused special football preview of the Ducks and the rest of the PAC.

The *RG* does a swell job in this year's roundup.

The self-aggrandizing moralist Canzano is nowhere to be found in this publication, so consider yourself lucky.

It's that time of year folks—my time.

SATURDAY, JULY 15, 2017

Depth?

This time of year I usually get revved up about the approaching college football season. I'm a little tame this year, but I'll probably be back to normal soon enough.

As I've written here before, the biggest drag for me is the way the business side of the game has taken over. But what can you do?

Big-time conferences get started with their month-long fall camps in about two weeks, so the 2017 season is rapidly approaching.

If you've followed this blog even casually since I started it in 2010, you know I'm an Oregon Ducks' fan.

Of course it is widely known that Oregon fell off last year after a decade-long stretch of winning seasons that included two national title games—both losses unfortunately.

The former staff didn't recruit enough good players on the defensive side of the ball in recent years, but offensively the Ducks were their usual dynamos.

So the old staff is gone, but the same defensive players are back. It could be a rough first year for new head coach Willie Taggart. Every game will likely be a shootout, which is a risky way to collect wins.

TUESDAY, DECEMBER 13, 2016

Rah, Rah

One could contend that just a tad bit of disrespect was shown toward Helfrich and his program after a 4-8 season that included some blowouts but also close losses to Nebraska, Colorado, California and Oregon State.

Mullens needed 72-hours after the Civil War loss to think about Helfrich's future, while the coach and assistants recruited for the Ducks? Wrong.

The UO sports information department needed to post a Helfrich firing story replete with details of the coach's downfall? Wrong!

And, in my humble opinion, the most egregious disrespect happened at Taggart's news conference when Michael Schill, a law professor and university president, said he had one piece of advice for the new coach, based on his limited knowledge of football: "Go find a great defensive coordinator."

Brady Hoke, the outgoing defensive coordinator, didn't deserve such a public slap in the face. UO's defensive woes happened because of youth, suspect recruiting and development, and player transgressions, and not just from schemes and play calls. It was just the wrong thing for the school president to say. Lacked class.—JV

Ducks' beat writer Jason Vondersmith of the *Portland Tribune* nails it when he says the UO brass showed disrespect and a lack of class throughout the firing and hiring process (portlandtribune.com Dec. 13, 2016).

I would add the brass showed a level of confusion that shouldn't have been there.

With what Oregon has coming back, Taggart will be an immediate villain in the opinion of Oregon's savage fans if he doesn't go at least .500 next year. Even that might not be enough to stymie the grumbling of the most idiotic.

FRIDAY, NOVEMBER 11, 2016

Stupor Bowl

Not into the Stupor Bowl this year for some reason, and I've never been a big "fan" of watching the glitzy new commercials that occupy many viewers.

Don't feel like joining the crowd. So I'll sit home and stream it if I can.

I'm definitely not into the hype. It's not Oregon football so I'm kind of like, what's the big deal?

Ho hum...

SATURDAY, NOVEMBER 29, 2014

Stuffed and Ready

I certainly had a good holiday. Hope you did as well.

This is going to be—what else?—a long day of college football-gazing as the regular season closes out before the conference championships kick off next weekend.

I'm ready for all the big matchups, not the least of which is the OSU vs. Oregon game from Corvallis this evening.

Before then, I want to glimpse some of the others; notably, tOSU vs. Michigan and FSU vs. Florida, which are like the local rivalry inasmuch as you can toss records out the window. These types of contests are always closer in the end than the on-paper-talent would indicate they should be, often going to the wire.

Bizarre things have and can happen, and with my Ducks playing for a spot in the inaugural CFP, I'll be on the edge of my seat. I'm personally on upset alert.

I'm focused. I wonder if my alma mater will be.

On a superstitious note, I don't like it that people are already talking up next weekend's Arizona and Oregon championship game in Santa Clara.

The Ducks have too much hard work scheduled for this evening to be thinking about that. It could be that UCLA fell into that trap yesterday, losing to Stanford.

All the talk leading up to that game was about how UCLA might win out and slip into the playoff. Stanford, a rugged team, had another notion.

The talent is too equal around the conference to expect anything to come easily.

All that stated, I expect Oregon to be focused, having learned the perils of not being as such in the recent past—too many times, in fact.

After that, it's a matter of which way the ball bounces.

FRIDAY, FEBRUARY 16, 2013

Chef de Cuisine

Yes sir, I made some soup last night that reminded me of the expertise I gathered in a dozen kitchens over the years.

I'm a little rusty these days, but I can do it if I bear down.

I was known for my good soup in the old neighborhood, where I worked for 16 years in the restaurant trade.

No less a luminary than Bob Costas praised my soup once in a neighborhood joint where I was working during the NBA Finals back in the Trail Blazers, Clyde Drexler glory years.

Called me to his table and said, I quote, "That is the best vegetable beef soup I've ever eaten."

I swear.

Another time, Oregon football coach Rich Brooks stopped by the service window in the same joint and praised the meal he'd just eaten, telling me the soup was especially good.

Last night I made a pot of an old standby, Cream of Broccoli and Mushroom. Shopping for ingredients, I was unaware of the current price of heavy cream because I never cook with it these days, so I went cheap and used half and half.

This batch wasn't celebrity-worthy, but it was still very good.

Not great, mind you, but man o man...

***

This is almost comical in its vagueness and subjectivity.

But the Playoff Committee is smart and has the answers, right?

Wrong.

I reiterate—and I'm far from alone in this—that the four-team playoff for the college national championship is a cruel joke.

My discontent is not based on the Oregon factor, either, since I'm a big Duck honk. All the Ducks have to do is win three down the stretch.

Quack, quack...

What I'm saying is that some very good one-loss teams will suffer this method like a beauty queen who is the third runner-up in a Miss America pageant Everybody in the ballroom will have an opinion.

The tears of rage will supplant the tears of joy among some very pretty women—er, teams.

The Oregonian's Ken Goe put it best earlier in the season:

I've been saying from the moment the College Football Playoff was unveiled, that it is as bad as or worse than the old Bowl Championship Series. It's a thinly-veiled way for the good ol' boys to keep their greedy fingers wrapped around college football's money and influence.

It's an exclusive system, standing in stark contrast to the NCAA Basketball Tournament, in which everybody, large and small, gets a shot.

If the powerful oligarchy that runs college football really wanted to determine a true national champion, this thing would be settled on the field in a real playoff.

I favor 24 teams. All conference champions would get an automatic berth. There would be eight, first-round byes. If the two best teams are from the SEC, well, let that be proven between the lines.—KG

SUNDAY, SEPTEMBER 21, 2014

Boobs

It's interesting reading some of the apocalyptic comments about the Ducks below the game stories in the local press.

The voices are amazingly persistent among conservative boobs. Many are the same posters, identifiable by their made-up names, who inform readers in other contexts that Monica Wehby is a good candidate for the US Senate, that food stamp cheats are a colossal problem, and that the US needs to nuke the Middle East, while gun rights are in peril across the land.

These people think McCain, Palin and Boehner are bright and their basic take on Oregon football is that Helfrich and Pellum "need to go."

The idiocy is funny, though somewhat sad.

Post-postpartum-mortem...

The faux football pundits are out in force this morning blaming Oregon's staff for a close win against what I believe is a very under-appreciated Washington State team and a QB who can make all the throws.

It boils down to this. Oregon's defenders just aren't as good as they need to be. You can teach tackling in space until your head falls off, but if the students don't respond because they don't have the innate gift, what are you going to do?

"If only Chip were here..."

If only Oregon's fans could come back to Earth...

Gonna be a long season.

SUNDAY, JUNE 1, 2014

Dog World Redux

I've added a segment about Multnomah Stadium to my baseball history (The Children of Vaughn).

The Beavers played in the stadium from 1956 onward, after the sale and razing of Vaughn Street Park.

In 1926 the Multnomah Athletic Club expanded its original (1893) sports field on land leased in the Tanner Creek Gulch neighborhood adjacent to Goose Hollow. This was a huge, privately funded project. It brought the seating capacity high enough to make major-college football an annual event in Portland for decades.

The Oregon Ducks (Webfoots) and Washington Huskies clashed there often.

In 1931, the Oregon Legislature legalized parimutuel betting in Oregon and the Multnomah Kennel Club started a regular program of greyhound racing at the stadium, which lasted until the Beavers moved in and the dog racing moved to Portland Meadows.

Multnomah Stadium became Civic Stadium when the city of Portland purchased it in 1966 for $2 million. In order, it has subsequently been renamed, in the indiscreet art of corporate advertising/sponsorship, PGE Park, Jeld-Wen Field and, currently, Providence Park.

Here is what has happened. PGE was purchased by Enron and ripped off many Portland retirees in a major corporate scandal you may recall. Jeld-Wen went into bankruptcy. Providence is a major HMO that rips off health consumers, which begs the question: How do you like it that your health care is a commodity?

Tonight, the Portland Timbers are warming up in the stadium for their futbol match with Vancouver. I can hear the 20K-plus futbol-crazed crowd chanting.

Portland remains a minor-league town, despite what is sold.

The Timbers wear the name "Alaska Airlines" on their jerseys, like that'll make them as good as a Euro team. But in some of our eyes it's all a bad joke.

SATURDAY, NOVEMBER 30, 2013

Bad Coaching

This day has been filled with nothing but bad coaching across the football world, and after yesterday's display of bad coaching by both Mike Riley and Mark Helfrich here in Oregon I am ready to give up on American football and coaching in general.

(Maybe I'll switch to soccer, an exquisitely boring game.)

All the bad coaching is making me sick, along with the bad analyses by the football pundits.

Witness what happened today in Auburn (Auburn returned Alabama's long field goal attempt for the game-winning TD). Now wasn't that a sickening display!

All I can say is Nick Saban needs to go because he lost a game he should not have lost, which makes him what—a loser!

WEDNESDAY, SEPTEMBER 4, 2013

The Meaning of Life

Let's be honest, there is no other reason to live but for Oregon football.

WEDNESDAY, AUGUST 28, 2013

Weekend

This weekend's college football schedule shapes up nicely. Oregon plays at 1 p.m. Oregon State starts at 3 p.m. Both games are televised. Both are playing patsies.

The two hours separating the games fits an Oregonian's schedule perfectly. Watch the first half of the Oregon game, which is about all any normal person will be able to tolerate, before switching to the OSU game.

The second game ought to be more interesting for a longer period of time, but both games could be over by halftime.

Scour the land and TV dial for another game.

The first game tomorrow (Thur.) features North Carolina vs. Jadeveon Clowney and South Carolina, nice start to the season.

I'm like a ten year-old with this stuff. Love it.

I guess I've never grown up. Doesn't mean I won't have my copy of *Gulliver's Travels* with its scholarly annotations beside me. Means I probably won't crack it real soon.

TUESDAY, JUNE 25, 2013

Better Late Than Never

It's about time.

Per Moseley's blog at the *Register Guard*, the NCAA will announce its findings, sanctions, against the University of Oregon football program tomorrow morning.

I can't wait.

MONDAY, SEPTEMBER 10, 2012

Sports News

John Boyett, an All-American is down and out for the season.

ESPN's Ted Miller says it's a worrisome situation. He's right.

Losing Boyett, a leader on the Oregon squad, is huge. In fact, the injuries are piling up in Eugene. It's somewhat freakish, as the guys getting hurt are upperclassmen whose proven skills should have carried the team.

'Tis true—you can count on nothin' in football.

The youth movement is on full-bore now and the PAC is suddenly looking tougher with the emergence of several teams that, given reality, could give my Ducks a go-round.

UCLA is one, obviously, after torching Nebraska. Fortunately the Ducks won't play them this season unless they knock USC out of the South Championship and Oregon wins the North.

That happened last year in fact, because the Trojans were on probation and UCLA backed into the title game.

OSU looked like a dominant defensive team against Wisconsin, though I still can't see Mannion as a force at QB.

Arizona looked flat out scary, running hard to the ball on defense and showing excellent overall team speed. Like UCLA's QB Brett Hundley, Arizona's QB Matt Scott looks fast and plays smart.

Arizona State also slapped Illinois, but it's hard to evaluate that game. Illinois is bottom tier these days.

Importantly, it is hard to evaluate my team as well. Its two opponents have made Oregon look bad on a few occasions but didn't have the horses to truly threaten the status quo.

TUESDAY, AUGUST 28, 2012

The Me Generation

Bryan Bennett, newly anointed backup quarterback to Marcus Mariota on the University of Oregon football team, is in a funk.

He's mulling a transfer.

Where?

When?

The better question is, why?

Marysota could break a leg in the first quarter of the first game of the year! Kids today are too selfish. It is all about me and me and me.

Wait — that's "Mariota could break a leg in the first quarter of the first game of the year! Kids today are too selfish. It is all about me and me and me."

Kid ought to stick around for this year, assess things and then make a decision. Hell, he could play for a Division III school next year and still catch on in the NFL.

It's not like the scouts don't know his talent level.

Jesus, I knew this would happen.

MONDAY, JANUARY 10, 2011

Trade Tools and Football

Spent the weekend resolving some technical/machine issues, culminating in what amounts to a fresh start, with excellent tools to continue and enhance the adventure known as Round Bend Press.

To quote the great David Byrne: "This ain't no foolin' around."

I'm looking forward to the BCS Championship game tonight. At least I think it is tonight. I heard Oregon is in it, so I might as well watch and see how Nike U. fares.

Hate Nike, love the team, which is a little like saying, hate the Military-Industrial Complex, but love the soldiers.

Personally, I think the Ducks' flashy uniforms will so stun Auburn that the SEC team from Alabama will not know how to respond to the beauty of it all while succumbing to a latent desire to dress like LaMichael James.

Plus Oregon is fast enough to get around the big beasts from the east and into the end zone numerous times.

Cam Newton will get his yards.

But Kenjon Barner, James and De'Anthony Thomas will get more—Oregon 37-30. (I was wrong.)

TUESDAY, SEPTEMBER 7, 2010

Labor Day with Mobutu and Football

Kind of a long weekend, wasn't it? I'm not a big holiday celebration guy to begin with, and it seemed like this weekend lasted forever. The day closed a couple of libraries, which cut into one of my favorite things to do— browse the shelves for interesting things to read without every actually reading them.

I've found a book about Mobutu Sese Seko, the onetime dictator of Zaire (Congo). Interesting and a good read, but I don't like the rhythm of its title, "In the Footsteps of Mr. Kurtz."

My Sunday training session for the podcast radio show was cancelled. That's one reason the weekend tended to drag. I was psyched to train and it didn't happen. I went to a pub and made a few notes instead. My radio mentor had a BBQ to attend.

I can't say that I blame him for the switcheroo.

I'm not ready to take the broadcast reins yet, particularly given what I want to do with Round Bend Hour down the road. I'll have to ease into the tech and its functionality, attempt to avoid dead air, etc. That means I'll start with a lot of music before upping the content. Get my "air" legs.

I have a feeling the Oregon/Tennessee game Saturday will be close. New Mexico had no business being in Autzen Stadium last weekend when Oregon smashed the Lobos.

In front of 102,000 in Knoxville, the Ducks will be challenged. It could be a "trap" game. It'll be interesting to see how the Oregon staff implements the Barner/James tandem on offense. Will Oregon be over confident?

I watched Boise State and Virginia Tech last night—the best game of the weekend. The programming experts at Disney nearly always get these high profile games right. Thanks ESPN. I'd like a job, please.

WEDNESDAY, AUGUST 23, 2017

Football is Back

I've been doing my football research the last couple of days.

The Pac-12 is quarterback country. Always is. Because the QB is always the most important player on any team, it's tough to say how the conference will play out. The champs always have good QBs, and there are some fine ones in the west.

Sam Darnold at USC, Josh Rosen at UCLA, Jake Browning at Washington, Luke Falk at WSU, Oregon's Justin Herbert—these guys can all play.

Who has the best supporting pieces then?

You start with your best players, but because injuries always manifest, you'll never know how deep you are until some of your young, unsung players have to do the job.

The supporting cast is crucial. If I were betting I'd take USC, despite the Trojans having what is perceived as a lack of depth. But we know they have good players. Experience counts; if the youngsters are forced into the game they'll likely shine from the get go.

So USC will be the Pac-12 champs.

Oregon? I think 6-6, with 8-4 as their ceiling.

It's real. The time is now.

THURSDAY, OCTOBER 15, 2015

Watchable

And so another football weekend begins...

I'm looking forward to UCLA vs. Stanford tonight. Somebody needs to beat Stanford or they'll walk off with another PAC title eventually, unless...

Unless the dreaded Utes of Utah take them out in Santa Clara, Dec. 5 in the PACCG.

Lots of football left though, including Alabama and A&M in the SEC.

Notre Dame and USC will be interesting for obvious reasons.

Washington will be sky high for Oregon Sat. night, savoring a realistic shot at beating the Ducks for the first time in twelve tries. Washington is favored, so maybe struggling Oregon will play better as the disrespected underdog...

Or, if a guy had a few extra bucks and a yen for live ball, PSU hosts Montana State Sat. at the perfectly reasonable 12:30 hour. PSU is playing well this season and a nice crowd will likely materialize at Providence Park.

Go Viks!!

Much else, including more baseball is on tap as well...all of it more enticing than televised "debates" or their inane cousins, the television sitcom.

WEDNESDAY, SEPTEMBER 23, 2015

Football Follies

As Yogi (R.I.P.) might have put it—*if it's not one thing, then it must be something else.*

First it was the struggle with Vernon Adams' math test from hell, which he finally passed. Now it is the case of the mysterious broken finger that plagues his presumed All-American year.

Oregon can't escape the drama at this stage. Play the damaged Adams, or the less-than-gifted backup, Lockie?

Tough call. I wish the staff best with this one as the Ducks prep for Utah on Saturday evening.

There is one thing I've noticed about Oregon's legion of football fans/experts, however—they will not be happy, no matter the outcome.

SATURDAY, SEPTEMBER 27, 2014

Game Report

Iowa State vs. Baylor better than Washington State vs. Utah.

WSU spent its wad on Oregon. ISU is pretty good, but so is Utah.

ED: Oh for god's sake. I've seen better football at a futbol match!

I joke. It's fun just watching the futility.

The dogs are both down by two TDs. Not a bad night for a football watcher. I'm entertained at the moment because both of these games are still in doubt.

Later: Nice comeback win by WSU. I know they're better than people give them credit for. They proved that against Oregon last weekend.

SUNDAY, MAY 25, 2014

Surviving the Indy and Vortex

I don't know how in the hell it happened, but I was a big fan of the Indianapolis 500 when I was a kid. Maybe every kid was in those days, but in hindsight you tend to wonder why.

I must have listened to the race on the radio in the days before it was televised, and I know Sports Illustrated always gave it full-coverage, so perhaps those were the key elements to my fascination early on.

I did love the look of the cars, and likely fantasized about driving very fast around and around an oval track. I wasn't a gearhead by any stretch, so I know the technical stuff involving these specially-built cars wasn't part of it.

It must have been purely the flash of speed and color, the essence of which was drawn out in those incredible SI photos that accompanied the Indy racing stories. I also had a fondness for Formula 1 racing. That one I appreciated more because the race courses ran through certain European and South American cities. That was very appealing from a visual standpoint, which must have been part of it—speed and interesting architecture in combination.

In 1970, after attending college in Ashland, Oregon for a year, I moved to Albany, an armpit of a town famous for its stinky industry and not much else sitting squarely in the the I-5 corridor. A new community college had just sprung up there, fashioned out of modular trailers before the campus had even broken ground. Since my mother had moved there after I finished high school in close-by Sweet Home, I commandeered her screen-enclosed front porch and moved in, transferring my shaky academic records from Ashland.

Then, as now, the community college was an outlet for the poor in funds and academics. I was on academic probation in Ashland, having not bothered to do anything except play football and drink while following my friends to the occasional antiwar symposium or rally.

I slept on my mother's porch and froze my butt off during the cold and rainy winter months, but when spring came around I had two more fairly solid terms of college under my belt and looked forward to transferring to the University of Oregon the next fall. I also played basketball and baseball for the first-year school, which kept me occupied as I worried about the draft that was still in affect at the time. I had a student deferment and definitely wasn't interested in going to Vietnam, so I studied and got my grades up.

I'd bought an old beater from my brother-in-law for fifty dollars so I could transport myself out to the community college at the edge of town. The beater's driveline would fall out eventually, stranding the car on a short access street between two of Albany's busier arterials near the railroad tracks, an occurrence that cost me a night in jail (another story). Until then the car served its purpose, however.

I drove it to Portland once, a risky adventure because the car wasn't freeway-worthy, like a moped isn't road-worthy. It spewed a little oil. It rattled and shook violently until it exceeded 60 mph, and it certainly was unsafe at any speed. But, you see, I just had to see the closed-circuit broadcast of the 1971 Indy 500 that I'd heard would be simulcast at Memorial Coliseum, a twelve thousand-seat basketball and hockey arena. It's where the Trail Blazers played before the Rose Garden, now the Moda Center, was built in the 1990s.

I remember being excited about the trip, despite its risks. I was determined to see the race for the first time, start to finish, but I soon found myself disappointed—for a number of reasons.

The crowd was extremely sparse, just a few morons hanging out. Somehow I'd pictured a full house of diehard racing fans. The grainy picture on a thirty-foot wide screen viewed from the back end of the seating area was in black and white. From where I sat, the screen seemed tiny. Hell, I could barely see it. I must have projected in my mind that it would be expansive, like a modern football replay screen in today's stadiums. I envisioned it covering an end wall inside the arena, I guess. The thought that it would be in black and white didn't occur to me, either. Colored TV hadn't been in existence very long at the time, but it was ubiquitous and improving annually. I expected color, dammit!

It was the beginning of the end of my interest in the Indy 500.

I watched half the race and got out of there. On the way home, I drove that beater way too fast.

I'd taken the beater on a previous risky trip, to the 1970 Vortex I gathering, where I camped for a night and recall being blown away by a rock band from Vegas called High Voltage. I rode with a bag of bad pot, but once at the festival I found the good stuff.

When the driveline fell out of that car, I went to jail. I'll spare you the details of that for now, but I'll tell you this much. I'm glad the driveline didn't fall out when I was speeding up and down I-5 as a dumbass kid seeking some of life's greatest pleasures. I guess I was lucky in that regard. I lived to watch more college football.

WEDNESDAY, OCTOBER 2, 2013

Restructuring (Paying Athletes)

The iron grip of the NCAA is about to be loosened.

The truth is I don't know the answer to this dilemma, but some sort of payday is in order. The biggest snag involves how most college sports, chained to the NCAA by Federal Title IX legislation and other regulations, become part of the equation if a form of disbursement is created.

How will it be implemented?

Football and basketball, the major revenue-generating sports at the big schools, finance myriad other teams across the board. Swimming, rowing, wrestling, baseball, etc., do not generate sustainable income at most schools, except in rare circumstances.

The baseball coaches at both Oregon and Oregon State have created strong programs of late, for example, but neither is self-sufficient. They rely on the revenue generated by football and basketball contracts with the networks, ticket sales, merchandising, and even some donor money.

In a true laissez-faire system unprofitable sporting events, like any other controlled endeavor, wouldn't exist. But that is not our system, despite what certain politicos would like you to believe. If it was, Wall Street would have been done in 2008 and the entire concept of the "public good" in society would implode instantaneously.

This deal will be interesting to follow, and finding a satisfactory solution will be difficult. Some argue college sports need to be abolished, except at the club level.

Perhaps that is where we'll ultimately land.

But good luck until then.

Heck of a football Saturday. Everybody lost except Oregon and Oregon State.

That's the way we like it, rah...rah...

SATURDAY, AUGUST 14, 2010

Saturday Notes

I worked all morning at designing the interior pages of memoire, *A Marvelous Paranoia*. Did some editing last night, but I wish I had a top pro working over my manuscript? I think it's improving but not nearly there yet. I inserted a title header on every page this time, which sharpens the book's overall look. Used a William Stafford quote and dedicated the book to my daughter and her son. I also explained that I changed some names in the book to protect the innocent.

Found a nice photo of a trumpet for my logo. I've used a trumpet logo in several of my designs, so I'm staying with the theme. I played trumpet years ago. I can still play, but my chops are practically non-existent. You don't forget how to play of course, but if you forget to practice you are doomed. "You've got to practice..." the trumpet-playing character in my play *Litany in a Trumpeter's Bog* advises, "Be like Miles."

I live near Portland State University, and I've been watching the Viking football team practice. The players seem small, Jerry Glanville's recruits for the *run and shoot* offense he and Mouse Davis implemented here last year. New football coach Nigel Burton doesn't have the players he needs to compete with the big boys.

Arizona State and Oregon and likely U.C. Davis will crush these guys. So will Montana. I might go to that game. It will not be pretty. The ASU and Oregon games will be nice paydays for the university, but someone may get hurt out there.

I liked the run and shoot. I saw Mouse run it in the early eighties during his first stint with PSU, with Neil Lomax at quarterback. I watched PSU play Delaware here in town. I think Lomax threw for eight TDs. The score was 102-0. Lomax had a short, injury plagued NFL career, but he was a special player.

I once interviewed Mouse and his staff about the run and shoot offense for a piece I was working up for Willamette Week, which didn't make it into the rag.

I watched an old man selecting tomatoes out of bins at the Farmers' Market on the PSU campus today. He was being very selective. I mean very, very selective. I didn't know one could obtain that kind of intensity regarding tomatoes. He was funny, about 90.

I don't know if it's a good thing to live that long, not that I have a chance. Probably don't eat enough tomatoes.

The PSU summer graduation ceremony happened earlier. I watched hundreds of newly minted college grads lining up to receive their sheepskins at Hoffmann Hall. It was already hot and most of them were carrying their gowns draped over one arm until they could get into the air-conditioned building to dress for the show. I strolled close to a group of them and asked if they were lined up to apply for unemployment benefits.

They laughed.

SUNDAY, FEBRUARY 11, 2018

RIP, John Thomas (1951-2018)

In high school John pitched for South Salem and worshiped the New York Yankees before heading off to college in Ashland, where our first encounter was on the Administration Building lawn when he quarterbacked a pickup football game and I tried to block for him on the line and somehow caught him in the eye with an elbow. As eye injuries go, it was pretty bad.

He went back to his room in Forest Hall and I later knocked on his door to apologize and Bob opened the door and I thought for a second that he was John and I said something, awkwardly confused, as Bob opened the door wider and I saw John lying on his bed face down nursing his injured eye. I said, "man I'm sorry," and he sort of grunted acknowledgement and I walked back to my room feeling bad that I'd hurt the guy.

Later, we became roommates in Forest when Bob moved into another room. John and Bob became my peer mentors in music, literature, politics and carousing, and there was, in my case, little time to study as I learned how to smoke pot for the first time and protest the Vietnam War.

John and Bob both laughed when I used "them" for "those" in conversation and once responded to a prof's question about why I was in his Psychology 101 class by answering in all sincerity that I wanted to know what "makes people tick." How was I supposed to know that I sounded like a hick to them?

John smoked cigarettes (a habit he would later quit when he took up long-distance running) on his bed in our college dorm room and read sociology and Vonnegut and crushed math problems that made my head spin because math wasn't my thing. He loved John Brodie and the 49ers and told Bob that Brodie was a better quarterback than Roman Gabriel, whom Bob preferred because Gabriel played for the Rams, Bob's team, and I made my case for Joe Namath and the Jets and we watched football on Sundays and drank beer all the time if we could get our hands on a case, and the truth is I couldn't stop laughing when I was around the twins because they were seriously funny guys whose sense of the absurd and general irreverence about everything made everyone around them laugh.

I had no discipline as a student and nearly flunked out by the end of third term and so I didn't return to Ashland for a second year, knowing I'd miss the brothers. But fortunately they went home to Salem for the summer and John always had an old runner that he'd drive down to Albany where I was living and pick me up to cruise up to Portland with them or up to Salem to hit the record stores and drive around for the hell of it. When Woodstock came out that summer we smoked so much pot that I was freaking out and in awe of the musicians and music on the big screen, and that was how I discovered John had learned Country Joe's "Fixin' to Die Rag" well enough to lead a sing along during a kegger at Emigrant Lake during my first and final spring session at Southern Oregon College. John had kicked it off and everybody at the party except me seemed to know the lyrics by heart and the singing was raucous and loud and echoed through the hills surrounding the lake and I thought, damn, I'm gonna miss this place, this school, "them" times.

But we watched Woodstock and had fun that entire summer, 1970. There's so much more I could write about. Perhaps I will in time, in the future.

I still write Bob on occasion and have published numerous of his photos at my blog, and I know John was a good photographer as well, and I learned a few years back that

John and Bob had both taken up biking with a passion, and I knew they both liked heading into the hills to ride.

That's what John was doing when he died, riding hard, staying in shape, seeking thrills where he could find them on a trail atop a mountain. It was a great scheme, a beautiful thing to do, and I'm just goddamn sorry it ended like it did, with a crash on a trail that looks pretty innocent in photos, except for the dip in the middle that John had flown over many times before--that is before Monday, Feb 5, when it happened. Despite wearing a helmet, John died of a blunt force injury to his head.

John was a good man, a good businessman, a loving husband to his wife of many years, Lori. He was great brother to his sister Colleen. He was Bob's best friend. He was my friend, and I feel terrible.

Rest in peace, John Edward Thomas, Jr. I loved you, man.

FRIDAY, MAY 13, 2016

The Risks

In the case of a massive earthquake you might be tempted to bend over and kiss your ass goodbye, depending on where you live or work. Don't be afraid.

It will happen here in Portland, Oregon someday. It's best to plan ahead.

I live on the fourth floor in an old brick apartment building reinforced in 2010. The dwelling made a city-issued list of "possibly" dangerous Portland buildings in the event of a catastrophic quake.

Never trust bricks in these situations.

The deal for me personally is that when the quake comes my building will collapse into its basement and I will survive the free fall, probably with a few broken bones, but mostly intact.

At times I lie in bed at night and think about it. My mattress and I will plunge down suddenly and forcefully, but the mattress will break my fall against the debris. Depending on how the ceiling and roof above me breaks down, I'll have a real chance to survive.

Bricks won't be the problem for me then, but rather that monstrous HVAC system that is directly overhead. I'll have to dodge that baby at the precisely right moment.

A few cuts and scrapes along with the broken bones would be a small price to pay for survival. I'll take the deal when and if it happens, perhaps with a quick rolling maneuver I learned in football.

To be cautious, I always wear a football helmet to bed, like BD in the Gary Trudeau cartoons.

FRIDAY, AUGUST 7, 2015

Golden Boys

Call it "tradition."

While a student at Oregon, I made sure not to miss a college football game in the early '70s (even at the expense of not studying on Saturday for a Monday quiz). Since then, I've always followed the careers of ex-Ducks in the NFL.

Since then I've watched the stars come and go, never up close like I did in my college years. I'm not a booster in that sense, don't give money for access. I don't call the coach at home in the middle of the night and bitch about the play-calling or the losing streak.

But I follow the players' post-Oregon careers.

I'm looking forward to watching Mariota try to make his mark in the league this year, just as I have in the past with Dan Fouts, Chris Miller, Akili Smith, Kellen Clemens, Joey Harrington, etc.

None of the others won the Heisman like Mariota, though Fouts is in the pro Hall of Fame. The others didn't have a lot of success, though Clemens has been in the league for a decade. Harrington's backup at Oregon, A.J. Feeley had a long career as well.

Be interesting to see what happens.

SATURDAY, JANUARY 10, 2015

Football and Pot

A second player, not as big of a star as Darren Carrington but still a valuable member of the team, was left home when Oregon traveled to Dallas yesterday for Monday night's NCG.

The team's many injuries have not been a distraction because they are a part of the game, unfortunate but accepted to a degree. Bad luck happens.

Losing players to the NCAA's drug screening program is another story. This has to be affecting the players' mentality and preparation for the game.

I would guess they're all over the map on this in terms of their reaction and feelings. It can't help but diminish their focus.

Pot on any campus is not a surprise any more, if it ever was. Particularly at Oregon, a bastion of liberalism if one ever existed.

Football is behind the social curve on this issue. Pot is legal in a lot of places now, though the federal government is determined to fight that reality.

I think punishing football players for smoking pot is silly.

THURSDAY, DECEMBER 11, 2014

Awards

The annual college football awards show is on. St. Marcus has picked up two awards tonight with perhaps a third to come.

The Heisman is presented Sat. night. Mariota won the Davey O'Brien Award given to the nation's best quarterback.

(Later: He also won the Maxwell and Camp awards, both given to the "best player" in college football.)

The show is pretty lame, rife with poor attempts at humor, ESPN self-love, and awkwardness.

I'd like to see an athlete turn down an award one day, say something like, "No thanks, send some money to a person who needs it instead."

Anyway, that's enough hype for me.

Congrats to Oregon and St. Marcus.

SATURDAY, OCTOBER 25, 2014

Weekend

Ought to be a good day for football watching with the possibility of a few "upsets."

Looking forward to OSU and Stanford, Ole Miss and LSU, maybe a couple of others.

Oregon won, but that defense needs work. Cal's offense is as good as they come, but Oregon gave away a lot with poor tackling.

People will want to blame the coaches again, of course, but I put it on the players. If you haven't learned to tackle in space by now you probably don't have the ability to do so consistently, which means you're not a serious contender for the championship.

The 1.5 hours in the dental office yesterday wasn't as painful as I expected it to be.

That's what I call good news these days.

MONDAY, AUGUST 18, 2014

Halfway There

Oregon is at the mid-point of its pre-season football camp, and there are either fifty or sixty guys on the team who can really play, or everyone is being overly praised.

Position and depth-chart battles are playing out everywhere on the field and decisions on which freshmen need to redshirt (practice but not play in games until next year) are being extended through this the third week of camp.

The coaches have ideas, but nothing is firm. Seems they were a little surprised by the talent that showed up—in what sounds like a good way.

Nice problem to have if it's real.

I'm looking forward to the start of the regular season, of course.

I'm not looking forward to the loudmouths who will bitch if things don't go exactly according to plan. Oregon is highly ranked, and people put too much stock in that.

Love the team and the idea of sports in college, but boosters and know-it-all fans with untethered expectations are a real drag these days.

FRIDAY, AUGUST 8, 2014

Quack, Quack

Dos quacks.

Last night it was DAT'S show in the NFL with an 80 yard punt return for a score.

Tonight Josh Huff did his thing, running a kickoff back 102 yards for a TD.

Both played at Oregon last year, and both had good overall careers.

Lots of Ducks in pro ball these days, reflecting the success of the team in recent years.

Can Oregon keep it up? We'll see in about 20 days when the college football season opens.

WEDNESDAY, JULY 23, 2014

Pac-12 Media Day

I shouldn't say anything because I'm a horrible public speaker myself, but I've never heard a football coach as bumbling as Oregon's Mark Helfrich when he opens his yapper.

I simply cannot listen to the guy.

Chip Kelly was fluent, if smug and deplorably arrogant.

I miss Mike Bellotti. The guy was smooth and smart, which may explain why he was chosen to work for ESPN as a broadcaster after leaving Oregon.

SATURDAY, OCTOBER 26, 2013

Drum Rolls

It's nothing like the energy you'll find on campus at a major football university each week on game day, but I have to give Portland State an A for effort.

The Vikings play North Dakota this afternoon, and the school band is ambling past my place, drums rolling, headed for Jeld-Wen Field where it'll set up to entertain the five-thousand faithful who stream into the stadium for the game.

It's great to hear. I remember incredible days in Eugene long ago, even though Oregon usually had a pretty bad team back in the '70s. Game day was always special for those of us who could pull ourselves away from the textbooks long enough to enjoy the festivities.

That was never a problem for me, as football Saturdays in October were a big part of college life in my estimation. I loved those days and look back at them with fondness.

At least that aspect of my life didn't drift past unnoticed, which is something I cannot say about much else.

SATURDAY, NOVEMBER 24, 2012

The Football Blues

Stanford beat Oregon in double-overtime, knocking the Ducks out of the BCS picture-large.

Never has 11-1 felt so bad.

Oregon didn't get any help today. I never thought I'd feel this bad about a great season.

One of the best teams in the country is out of it. And goddamn, Notre Dame is beating USC.

Oh well, maybe next year.

I won't be happy until an eight-team playoff becomes the norm in college football.

Until then, the SEC computers will prevail and it will stink every year, just as it stinks now.

FRIDAY, NOVEMBER 23, 2012

Great Expectations

Late-season rivalry games are the best college football has to offer year in and year out.

Washington State was a dog this afternoon yet pulled out a wild win over Washington in Pullman. Tonight, Arizona State rallied late to knock off favored Arizona in Tucson.

The PAC is a crazy league and parity is the main reason. A longtime fan of rivalry games in the PAC, I've learned to expect the unexpected.

Today made for a fine start to a weekend of great expectations and entertainment.

Tomorrow should be even better.

I expect USC to unexpectedly knock over the favored Notre Dame Fighting Irish tomorrow in Los Angeles. I expect to see UCLA unexpectedly stun tough Stanford, also in L.A.

These expectations are sometimes referred to as prayers.

Unfortunately, I also expect an unexpected loss by Oregon to Oregon State in the Civil War, an expectation that I hope is wrong.

It's rivalry week across the country, the best reason I know of to watch T.V. and cuss like a madman.

MONDAY, NOVEMBER 12, 2012

Big Babies

Football news: Man, Oregon—my team in case you are unaware of it—is banged up in its defensive ranks. Against Cal the Ducks played three to five babies at a time along the defensive line—babies being my term for true freshmen.

The extended playing time for the big babies—and they are huge kids—will make them stronger in a year or two. Right now, however, I fear they won't have the strength/power to neutralize Stanford's upperclassmen along the line Saturday when the geniuses visit Autzen.

Oregon will have to score a ton in what I'm guessing will be the closest game the Ducks have had to date. Of course, Oregon has been pretty fair at scoring a ton all year...

Will Stanford slow down Barner and company?

WEDNESDAY, AUGUST 29, 2012

Oregon Promo

Oregon football is what it is all about from my perspective.

Bring the games on, starting tomorrow night when Mike Leach's Washington State team takes on BYU.

I can't wait!

***

Running a publishing empire like this one can be a tad stressful at times, but I have to say that today has drifted past with great ease and a sense of calm.

A rare day in that regard (and I know this isn't an empire, but I thrive on my lame jokes). I feel relaxed.

Generally I'm grinding, bursting with insecurities and confusion, and a sense of not knowing.

Today? Just living the life and hoping for the best.

Saturday evening, I took a number of long strides in learning the new RBP editing system that I eventually plan to use to produce what I hope are videos a notch-step above what I've created in the past.

A broadcast television pro who, as he describes it, works in the "belly of the beast," helped me enormously. We'll see what transpires with my new-found understanding, or what I hope is understanding and not another dead end.

Additionally, I'm editing another book.

That's going well. I think I'm a good editor, not of my stuff of course, but of other things that pass under my nose. This part of the job always levels me out somewhat. The nuts and bolts stuff that clears my head and helps me think I'm contributing something of value to the world.

What else is a man to do, I ask you? This is a racket after all, not unlike attempting to sell small figurines to equestrian-loving damsels.

Or a stack of baseball cards to a Cardinals fan.

BTW, I went over to Stott Field on the Portland State campus the other day and took in a Viking spring football practice, as has been my habit since moving into my nearby neighborhood a couple of years ago.

Maybe I'll post a little practice video here next week, like a football blogger.

I like what I see from the Vikings in the third season of Nigel Burton's coaching tenure. Burton has his players and system in now. I look for PSU to make the playoffs next November.

Burton has the team playing fast and focused. I'm not a big fan of Chip Kelly at Oregon, but his influence on the college game is readily apparent. Kelly is a big-time practice coach and his methodology has spread throughout the college landscape.

His mantra is "play fast, hard, and finish."

That's what we say here at Round Bend as well.

MONDAY, FEBRUARY 6, 2012

Noted

An entertaining Super Bowl, but not being a pro football fan in general (I like college ball), my heart wasn't in it.

The major difference between the pros and collegians is the sheer speed of the athletes. Even the huge guys have speed to complement their bulk and toughness.

I met up with Terence Connery, who is a television director and always has interesting production-related things to comment on during a telecast. A former Floridian, he covered the Dolphins and Marlins in Miami in the early 90s.

Poor guy is actually a big Dolphins fan. It's been a while for him...

Charles Lucas was also there, knocking back a few beers with Terence and me. Lucas is a solid barroom football analyst, given to grand pronouncements such as: "The coaching then was awful." And, "The refs are blowing too many calls." And, "It would have been more feasible to throw a pass then rather than run the ball for a three yard loss."

SUNDAY, JANUARY 22, 2012

Flu Bug

I just spent the entire day on my bed watching professional football.

And I'm not a pro football fan by any stretch of the imagination. But with these new flu symptoms I have—I'm not alone apparently—staying on the bed was about all I could muster.

I watched a guy miss a little chip-shot field goal in the first game. I'll bet he feels like shit, too. He could have sent the game into overtime.

He might get the flu tomorrow when he gets fired.

Or jump out a 10 story window in Baltimore.

Prior to the missed field goal, a receiver dropped a game-winning touchdown pass. Let a little cornerback strip the ball out of his arms. Sheesh...

In the second game, San Francisco's Kyle Williams made a couple of huge mistakes and helped the New York Giants steal an overtime victory.

Springsteen sang a song about one Kyle Williams back in 1983. Might be the same one, about the same age:

Take a baby to the river, Kyle William they called him
Wash the baby in the water, take away little Kyle's sin
In a whitewash shotgun shack an old man passes away
Take his body to the graveyard, over him they pray
Lord won't you tell us, tell us what does it mean
At the end of every hard earned day people find some reason to believe.—"Reason to Believe" from *Nebraska*

Poor Kyle Williams.

Poor Baltimore. A couple of my favorite old Oregon Ducks play for the Ravens. Haloti Ngata and Ed Dickson.

Better luck next year, guys.

THURSDAY, DECEMBER 22, 2011

A Year in the Life--Summertime

More on Round Bend's past year...

The living was easy over the summer as I assessed Round Bend's potential. K.C. Bacon's second book, *Morandi's Bottles*, went to press, followed soon thereafter by Charles Deemer's *In My Old Age*.

Both books were immediately assigned to RBP's Amazon pages, safely out of the hands of their meddling publisher.

I thought both books outstanding and sought to express as much here in my publisher's role.

In My Old Age was given deliberate scrutiny by the Pacific Northwest Booksellers' Association in consideration of its 2012 awards, dealing the press an unexpected shot in the arm.

Alas, it did not make the final cut, but as I explained to the chagrined author—the PNBA's decision shouldn't be construed as a vote against what he and I both knew—the book was first-rate, lacking only familiar poems about Oregon's deserts and mountains, flora and fauna, and sacred salmon—the stuff Snyder gave us fifty years ago. Something about aging has universality, whereas the Pacific Salmon doesn't always play well in Azerbaijan or Cairo—except as perhaps a very expensive food fish.

Deemer has, as football coaches love to say about a good linebacker, a non-stop motor. He soon took his poems to Lewis & Clark College to archive them at the Oregon Voices Project.

He also organized a reading at the Blackbird Wine Shop for October as part of the shop's monthly First Wednesday art venue.

It was around this time, too, that Charles informed me that his brother Bill was interested in publishing a print-on-demand book. Would I be interested?

At the risk of sounding overly poetic, I said, "Does a bear shit in the woods?"

I felt the summer was progressing swimmingly, in the direction of Oregon football, when I began to talk seriously with Charles Lucas about producing a book of his recent paintings.

FRIDAY, OCTOBER 28, 2011

Sports!!!

Get your popcorn ready. Game 7 of the World Series begins in 15-minutes.

I'll be switching between the Series and the BYU v. TCU football game. I need another computer or a TV, one or the other.

The football game is in Arlington. That's Texas Ranger territory. I wonder if anyone will go to the game.

Big night, but small potatoes compared with tomorrow's schedule. My Ducks at noon, Nebraska and Michigan State in the morning, Stanford and USC in prime time.

That last one is huge for Stanford if the Trees want to play in the NC this year, which would be cool if Oregon can't beat them.

I've always liked Stanford, my second favorite PAC team.

FRIDAY, SEPTEMBER 9, 2011

Time after Time

What happened to this week?

The days of this life stream past much too fast. What happened to my youth when I waited and waited for something to happen?

Hell, for that matter what happened to my middle age?

Now everything happens at once and it is suddenly Friday and I am old and feeling like it.

What did I do with the week? Well, I met with my landlord and talked about the terms of my tenancy.

I walked to the corner store Wed. night around ten and almost got robbed on the way home. A couple of punk Mexican kids came after me. I think one of them had either a knife or a gun in his pocket. The hand was definitely bracing something hidden. I warned them away. Warnings always create smirks on the faces of cowardly punks.

They kept coming. Fortunately I was near the porch of my building and scampered up the steps. I grabbed the lobby phone as they walked past the doors, watching me.

They hustled around the corner. I didn't call the police. They were looking for somebody to mug. I think I'll get a pistol for protection. The area of town I live in is getting sketchier by the day.

Things are happening. They're just happening too damn quickly.

I'm ready for the Blackbird reading though, starting with a short chapter from my memoir *A Marvelous Paranoia* titled "My First Beer." I think it's funny. We'll see what the crowd thinks, I guess. With a fifteen-minute reading slot, I'll also read a pair of my best poems from *Cello Music & Other Poems* if time allows.

Looking forward to a big weekend of football. Oregon State at 9 a.m. tomorrow morning. The Beavers are playing a very good Wisconsin team on ESPN, so it might get ugly fast.

My Ducks have Nevada a little later in the day. I see this one, after witnessing last week's Oregon debacle, as a tossup. Nevada was 13-1 last season. They have an outstanding coach and good talent.

We'll see.

SATURDAY, OCTOBER 30, 2010

Weird Feeling

I don't like the feel of the setup in L.A. tonight. Maybe I'm just a natural pessimist (there really is no maybe about it), but I think Oregon will fall tonight. I hope I'm wrong, but something just doesn't feel right.

Maybe I'll change my mind before kickoff.

Football fans are irrational. We put irrational hope in games—silly games of violence and speed. We sometimes forget the games are meaningless entertainments, something to fill the void in every fan's life.

For a very few the games are a livelihood, to be sure. But for most people, their value degenerates by bedtime.

This has been an extraordinary season for the Oregon program. I'd like to see its good fortune continue. We'll know more at bedtime tonight.

FRIDAY, OCTOBER 8, 2010

A New Era

I was reading somewhere recently that there are risks inherent in games between physically mismatched teams in developmental youth football.

No kidding.

Folks pay attention these days, but that certainly wasn't the case when I played high school football in the sixties. I played at a very small school in a league with schools three and four times larger than mine. My school might have a couple of big guys each year, but too few to make an impact on the overall competitive level of our squad. We were often thumped hard by teams with a lot of big players. Nobody cared that we were getting our heads bashed in by 6-6 280 pounders and losing by 60 points every game.

We were told it built character to be bullied so badly.

States now attempt to classify schools by their enrollments. Oregon now fields Classes 6 through 1 in descending order.

I wasn't really good enough to play big time college ball, but I played against many who were. I tried to survive in the main, and I was lucky to not get seriously hurt at various times.

Times have changed. Fear now rules—of injuries, lawsuits, etc. Maybe there is some good sense in there, too.

FRIDAY, SEPTEMBER 24, 2010

Week 4 (college football)

Now comes the big test for the Mighty Oregon Ducks as we get to see how good they are and can possibly be as the season progresses. They play ASU Sat. night.

The game will accentuate speed, a style the always big and lumbering Wisconsin Badgers had a dose of last week when ASU went to Madison and nearly (shoulda) beat the big cheese heads. WU has a monstrous offensive line and ASU countered with fast, aggressive linebacker play. Thus a low-scoring standoff that hinged on a couple of special teams errors.

ASU is good, make no mistake about it. ASU coach Dennis Erickson knows what he's doing, even if he did jump on the spread option bandwagon a tad late. He has the professional loyalty of your average heroin dealer, but what the heck.

I like Oregon, maybe short of the spread, which is -10.5. But I ain't bettin' it.

Other game winners and losers:

Arizona wins, but Cal plays better than it did at Nevada.

USC wins because WSU is inept.

OSU loses because Boise is very good.

Stanford loses in an upset to Jesus U. (Notre Dame)

UCLA cannot beat Texas in Austin.

If you have any questions phone Dooley's Betting Parlor and ask for Mo.

THURSDAY, SEPTEMBER 2, 2010

Kickoff!

The 2010 college football season begins tonight with its annual cupcake bake-off across the land. Perennial powers USC and Ohio State ease into the season with a pair of warm up games against Hawaii and Marshall respectively. USC, playing at Hawaii, is on vacation—a long one; they can't go bowling this year because they cheated so much over the past decade. They will play nasty tonight and beat up the Rainbows—er, Warriors.

Ohio State's Terrelle Pryor is a big quarterback and fine runner; I'm still not convinced he's a good passer, though. Marshall won't beat tOSU, however. A yawner in more ways than one. OSU's Jim Tressel is football's most conservative game planner. He always dresses in a sweater vest, too, a sure sign.

The best game of the night features Utah at home against Dion Lewis and 15th ranked Pittsburgh. Lewis is a supersoph running back like Oregon's LaMichael James and fun to watch. This game ought to be competitive, a chance to see how Utah shakes out as it prepares to jump to the Pac-12 (with Colorado) next year.

I won't be climbing any mountains tonight, or running any marathons, or even dancing the jig at the local dance hall.

I'll be getting my exercise on the sofa—a beer in one hand and a club sandwich in the other.

Life is good, I say.

SUNDAY, JUNE 6, 2010

Why I Did Not Go To Vietnam

Today is the sixty-sixth anniversary of D-Day, and the Greatest Generation is rapidly dwindling. We understand that fascism needed to be stopped, and we rightfully thank the many Americans who made it happen.

Few Americans would disagree with that sentiment. Or this one: Had Hitler's racism been confronted before his war machine was fully revitalized, he may have been stopped cold shortly after seizing power in 1933.

Hindsight is beautiful. We can and do learn from it at times.

That said, if you have followed this blog with even passing interest, you understand that I believe war is folly. Barbara Tuchman's history of war, *The March of Folly*, is a fine book, its title catchy and to the point. Wars, even the necessary ones, are folly.

Rudimentarily, we know why wars happen. We know they spring from inhumane impulses and ignorance. We know the corrupting nature of avarice and the geopolitical realities that propel conflict. We know that the lust for power is systemic, and that unrestrained nationalism plays a role.

At this late date, we understand the psychology of war.

But none of that sufficiently explains the neocolonialist impulse that sprang from post-World War II realities, particularly in the U.S. and Russia.

That impulse sat in front of us like a meal of strychnine laced with rat poison, yet we bit it off and chewed it down like candy.

France clung to Indochina, and was routed by a people seeking the ideal we supposedly fought for in Europe—actual freedom.

The hypocrisy astonished Graham Green, making it worthy of a novel, *The Quiet American*. Greene had seen the brutality of the French close-up in Vietnam, reporting for the *London Times* and *Le Figaro*. In creating quiet Alden Pyle, the naive and privileged American, Green wasn't about to let American treachery off the hook in 1955.

A decade later, the U.S. was in the shit up to its eyebrows in the Ia Drang Valley of the Central Highlands, South Vietnam.

Only fifteen at the time, I wasn't there. My brother, however, had served in Vietnam, in 1963 and 1964, building landing strips near the demilitarized zone between North and South Vietnam. At the time, his unit couldn't return fire when in-coming mortar rounds crashed inside his Marine battalion's position. You see, America was not yet officially in the war, although Americans were being killed.

Ia Drang changed that.

After I graduated from high school, in 1969, I moved to Ashland, Oregon, to attend college and play football. My school counselor had suggested I nab a deferment and go to college instead of joining the Air Force, which had been my vague plan before I talked to him. He had asked me why I was considering the Air Force, and I had told him the truth. I saw it as an alternative to the draft and the Army infantry.

I was not fully aware at the time that Air Force—and Navy—enlisted men were also dying in Vietnam.

We studied current events in 1969. My instructor never went into detail about the war. He was a cheerleader certain that crushing communism and blocking the falling dominoes in Southeast Asia was the right course. To please him, I wrote a paper on the evils of communism. I parroted his views, and he loved it.

I didn't believe any of what I'd written, because I had no idea what the hell I was talking about.

My teacher had not done me a favor by accepting my weak, uninformed effort, but I doubt even he understood what was happening.

It turned out I was as naive as Greene's Alden Pyle about Vietnam. Here's what I knew about Vietnam. I knew I didn't want to end up dead.

I have another example of how naive I was about the war. My mother hid a scary fact from me—actually, she simply lied to me. The entire time my brother was in Vietnam, she told me he had a desk job in Okinawa.

Maybe she wanted to believe that herself.

My mother did not want me to worry, for she worried enough for both of us.

My brother did ship back to Okinawa, unscratched, just before the Battle of Ia Drang Valley, in November, 1965, when the killing in Vietnam escalated. When he left the Marines a year later he didn't return to our small Oregon town, except to visit briefly before settling in the San Francisco area.

By the time I visited him in Fremont, south of Oakland, California, in 1972, he was married and the father of a baby girl. But something was wrong.

We stood in sharp political contrast. I had been radicalized in college and I hated the Vietnam War. My brother hated war protesters.

Thus began a long stretch of hostility between two brothers, born six years apart, but separated by a war and rapidly changing American culture.

I looked for a long time for the root meaning of our differences. I had become politicized in the middle of a great cultural change. When he joined the Marines in 1962, there were a few hundred American advisers in Vietnam, and any number of Alden Pyles. At first, what they were doing there promised to be a short-term job.

That the U.S. thought it might supplant the French and save capitalist imperialism in Southeast Asia was, of course, folly. Few Americans knew it, however. Six short years later, even Lyndon Johnson knew that many high school counselors in small town America considered Vietnam a quagmire and were advising their students to stay clear of it if they doubted the cause.

Mine had, without tipping his hand. All he said was think about it. That was enough.

I did not get drafted and go to Vietnam, or join the Air Force.

I did not suffer a pang of patriotism and volunteer to save America from communism.

I feared war—not communism.

I couldn't see the rationale for sending nineteen-year olds off to fight a war that was not clearly just.

I did not go to Vietnam because I did not want to kill people for a cause I knew nothing about.

I did not go to Vietnam because I did not want to be shot at for a cause I did not understand.

I did not go to Vietnam because I did not believe the cause was just.

Sadly, my fortuitous time was a tragic time for many young men in my cohort. As is this time, for many other young men and women. They are soldiers now... and young.

WEDNESDAY, DECEMBER 7, 2016

Willie Taggart/Give it Time

Kudos to Oregon for hiring an African-American coach with a record of turning programs around.

A first for the university in football.

Now we must watch and see if he is as good as his backers say he is, a group including Tony Dungy and the Harbaugh clan.

SATURDAY, NOVEMBER 12, 2016

From Bad to Worst

Jeez, I guess I was wrong about my Ducks winning today.

It's okay, I've been wrong about a lot of things lately. I'm not in favor of anyone losing a job, but I certainly have no say in anything.

This game might have saved the head coach, had his team performed. It didn't, and that is a sorry reality in these days of hyper-economic college football.

Oregon has a good young QB, however. But so did WSU for years while the Cougs struggled until this season.

Up next, USC and Washington. I'm listening right now.

Later, OSU and UCLA. I'll listen to a bit of that too, before crashing.

FRIDAY, DECEMBER 19, 2014

Raiders Become NAIA Champs

Southern Oregon University's football team is playing for the NAIA National Championship this afternoon.

Go Raiders!

Update: Won it. Never seriously threatened.

MONDAY, NOVEMBER 3, 2014

Mighty Presbyterian

The SEC's Mississippi schools are ready for their late-season break and fourth cupcake each on Saturday. This means their eight-game pseudo-competitive conference schedule is temporarily on hold.

Oh, and they each get another guaranteed win.

Praise Jesus!

Here's the lineup: Ole Miss gets Presbyterian.

Well, it's a good thing Ole Miss already has two losses, or this one could have put the Rebels in the championship game just because ESPN wanted them there.

And after polishing off a "tough" Arkansas club last weekend, 17-10, number one Miss. State gets to tangle with "tough" Tennessee-Martin (or something like that).

Upset city??

Meanwhile Oregon is playing Utah in a death match this Sat., and Pac-12 South leader Arizona State gets to play Notre Dame.

What say you, football fanatics? We're weeding out the Presbyterians and small-time Tennessee schools, aren't we?

I love it!

WEDNESDAY, OCTOBER 15, 2014

Many Moons Ago

Where were you the last time Washington beat Oregon in a football game? The year was 2003, in case you're wondering.

I was working as a fill-in night appetizer chef at the Saucebox, a bullshit hipster joint on Broadway in downtown Portland.

The scenesters were too hip to have a telly in the joint as they enjoyed their cocktails and boring conversations, so I had to hand my duties off to the other fill-in night chef and traipse across the street to a combo pizza hall and pool joint that had a couple of TVs blasting.

The game was in Seattle, and Washington tormented Kellen Clemens no end, beat the Ducks 42-10, I think.

It was a major disappointment, alleviated by my obligation to head back to the cafe and relieve my co-worker, who went off silently into the night.

I cleaned everything up and got out of there myself a couple of hours later.

And that was the last time UW beat the Ducks.

What will happen this Saturday? Only thing I know is I won't be serving a lot of crap appetizers to the rich asshole children of Portland's aristocracy, thank my lucky stars.

SUNDAY, AUGUST 31, 2014

Word of the Day

"Vanilla."

An obfuscation meant to express the fiction that Oregon's defense was hiding "schemes" and "packages" from its next opponent, and thus didn't bother to seriously challenge the South Dakota offense in a football game yesterday at Autzen Stadium in Eugene.

Not to be confused with "inept" tackling.

Or "disinterested" play.

Or "depleted" talent.

SATURDAY, JUNE 14, 2014

National Champs

Led by the superb Devon Allen, Oregon wins the NCAA Track and Field Championship for the first time in 30 years.

Allen practiced football and ran the hurdles this spring. Now the true freshman is the second-fastest U.S. 110 meters hurdles guy ever.

A potential Olympic-level two-sport star in the making.

MONDAY, MAY 19, 2014

Third Chance (Recently)

Being the bleeding-heart liberal that I am, I hope Colt Lyerla recovers from his disastrous exit from Oregon and makes a different name for himself in the NFL.

He's an Oregonian who grew up under, sniff, difficult "circumstances."

I've always rooted for underdogs, even the ones who have rubbed me the wrong way, or the ones with gifts they've squandered.

The trick to my own avoidance of trouble as an impoverished youngster growing up in Oregon was that I didn't know I was poor. Hell, I thought everybody ate government cheese by the pound, free of charge, and that not having dental work done when you needed it in childhood was the norm.

This was before ubiquitous expressions of privilege and middle-class expectations of comfort dominated the polity. We've gone full-circle, and now I do expect a level of comfort in my world, like everybody else.

Like Lyerla, I was fatherless. Even today I envy listening to others' talk about their lives with Dad, good or bad. Didn't happen for me, so any kind of basic role model, mentor, whatever, was out of the question. Perhaps I leaned too much on my childhood friends' fathers, but often times they were missing as well. Perhaps I've leaned too heavily on friends subsequently.

A good female friend of mine once labeled me a "malcontent." As I look back at things, I can't think of a better description.

I certainly don't feel any love for the "way things are."

Fortunately, I haven't had much trouble with the law in that regard. I think I've been lucky.

Some of us are simply born rebels, with nothing recognizable to fall back on. I write of this in my mainly unread partial memoir, *A Marvelous Paranoia*.

Others have called me cynical, whereas I prefer the more nominative handle—*confused*.

To be cynical projects something related to egoism. I'd have to have blind faith that I know something to begin with to achieve the sort of cynicism I see around me. The most cynical are the assholes with perfect vision, or worse, those with money, particularly those who haven't earned it, but have rather had it handed to them.

Step down, Mitt Romney, you dumb fucker.

I love being a malcontent. I'm not being cynical about this, either.

I understand Lyerla. I don't like cocaine, but he does (or did). The rest of it I can relate to. I understand his anger most of all.

The world doesn't need another ditch digger or insurance salesman or homeless beggar, even another would-be writer. If it needs another football star, I'm rooting for him.

***

Oregon's deeply delusional fans won't have Nick Aliotti to kick around anymore.

Anybody who actually knows football, as opposed to say bandwagon fans and would-be coaching philosophers, knows this guy was golden.

When he had the high-level defenders—and it is questionable whether he had them this year despite the obnoxious shit-spew of the seeming-to-know crowd—he was a force.

Last year, with Dion Jordon, Kiko Alonso and Michael Clay, Oregon's defense was a dominant unit.

What about the excellent defenders on the 2011 NCG team; Spencer Paysinger and Casey Mathews, you corrupted spoiled nincompoops.

A number of DBs who are having nice careers in the NFL right now, not to mention many others whose careers lasted until they aged out—you faux experts.

Haloti Ngnata?

On and on.

I loved Aliotti not only for his expertise as a DC, but as a comic and a wear-it-on-your-sleeve orator.

The guy was a fucking legend after 24 years in the program, and the punks out there don't even know it.

SUNDAY, DECEMBER 8, 2013

Play Nine or STFU

Goodness, what a boring football lineup for the bowl season.

Has a one-loss team—with two of the luckiest last-second wins in games it was better positioned to lose—ever been in the title game before?

Why Auburn? Why not Baylor? Why not Michigan State? The latter two might give FSU a game, but we'll never know.

Personally, I think Stanford is the best team in the country right now. FSU is number two, Alabama is number three, and Baylor is number four. MSU is number five.

Stanford, in this group, has two losses, but so what? It has the best defense in the country by far and plays in a conference that counts nine games.

The SEC counts eight. That means Auburn gets an extra patsy—four in all—on its schedule. This is the way the SEC works, via a process of avoidance.

This development is a farce, and a fitting end to the BCS era. Unfortunately, a four-team playoff commencing next year will be just as stupid.

Condi Rice will be calling the shots, so we know it'll have legitimacy...right.

Re: Oregon, I'm with Huff and DAT on this one. The Alamo Bowl is a drag. Who cares?

If I can pull myself out of bed by four in the afternoon on the 30th, I'll probably tune in.

If not, I'll just keep reading or scratching my balls.

But I wish I was a Beaver fan. OSU is going to Hawaii to play a meaningless game. I'd like to hitch a ride.

FRIDAY, NOVEMBER 15, 2013

Saturday Gig

Charles Lucas and I scored tickets to watch Portland State and Sacramento State tomorrow at Jeld-Wen.

Suite seats in the uppity-brow section, via one of my ex-employers. Old Lucas hasn't seen a football game live since Gayle Sayers ran like a hellion for the Bears back in the day. He's pumped.

I'm pumped. We'll catch some of the Oregon/Utah game on one of the TVs in the suite.

A few brews might be taken down as well.

Sounds like a good day ahead.

TUESDAY, NOVEMBER 5, 2013

Truants

I can't believe what I just read.

Stanford students to skip classes in preparation for the big game with Oregon Thursday night?

Up in Pullman last Thursday, WSU canceled classes for the day. But that is WSU, and evidently the parking situation on campus played into the decision.

Can't let those tailgate parties flounder now, can we?

Stanford isn't canceling classes, at least not officially, but this is starting to look like a trend for Thursday night football.

I hope that missed lecture doesn't come at too big a cost for some.

SATURDAY, AUGUST 31, 2013

What It Is

My goodness...

The Beavers fall. Thought they might handle EWU, but they simply didn't play defense. Tough to win that way.

Does OSU have enough to compete in the PAC? Not yet, for sure.

I thought Oregon's pass defense was a little leaky, probably due to the inexperience at linebacker. Terrence Mitchell was tossed for a "targeting" flagrant.

Dumb play.

He missed three quarters of the game. Hope he learned his lesson. The lesson is if you have any desire to hit a prone player on the ground, leading with your helmet, be advised: don't do it.

Good rule. I feel bad for Beaux Hebert, Mitchell's victim.

Nicholls was better than anticipated.

Mariota's speed seems to have improved. He's bigger now, too. Bralon Addison is a terror. Huff looks like he's ready.

Byron Marshall turned on the jets for a 50 yard TD run.

Dat took some hits and bounced up every time.

What a day of football! Better than I hoped for.

WEDNESDAY, JULY 31, 2013

PSU Camp Opens Thursday

Let us not forget about Portland State.

I went to school there also, so the Vikings are one of my teams. They dipped last season when I thought they might finally get over the hump after a decent 2011 campaign; I still think Nigel Burton can get it done in the Park Blocks.

In his fourth year at PSU, he's running out of time to do something and move up in the coaching ranks. If he doesn't prove himself this season he'll probably lose his job, and the Vikings will have to start anew once again.

We all know what that is like, right?

The team starts practicing tomorrow at 1 p.m. First game: Thursday, Aug. 29 at Jeld-Wen, with a 7 p.m. kickoff against Eastern Oregon.

Won't be much of a contest, but at least it will be a football game rather than soccer at the landmark old stadium that was gussied up by the Timbers ownership a few years ago.

The Timbers draw 20K a game. PSU will be lucky to get half that many to its opener.

FRIDAY, SEPTEMBER 28, 2012

Fear

Here is an interesting tidbit from the world of college football.

Oregon, ranked No. 2 in the latest polls, is dead last in the 124 team FBS standings in kickoff returns—despite having the wondrous De'Anthony Thomas fielding returns for the Ducks.

Through four games, nobody has kicked the ball to Thomas!

That is right. He hasn't returned a kick this year because the opposition is afraid to kick it to him.

But here is the deal. Mike Leach, the Washington State head coach, will throw all of that nonsense out the window tomorrow night; I'll bet you a dollar.

Leach is unconventional, a pirate, having dressed like one once.

Watch Thomas create a few long runs for fun tomorrow night in Seattle.

Leach has a three-year plan in place at WSU. Give him time. He won't back down.

THURSDAY, SEPTEMBER 27, 2012

Good Game

A funny football game in Seattle tonight as Washington knocked off No. 8 Stanford 17-13.

Oregon plays Washington State in Seattle Saturday night and should dominate.

Next weekend, Washington visits Eugene for what suddenly looks like a very interesting matchup.

This is what it is all about. The PAC is rolling!

FRIDAY, JULY 27, 2012

Big Bore

Olympic madness.

Not into it, though I'd be elated if Rupp, Eaton, et al., win medals. Oregon grads can do no wrong, you know?

In the past I might watch a little basketball, but I can't stand today's stars, so that is out.

As an event the Olympics have become too corporate and predictably maudlin for my tastes.

I want to be entertained. I'll bear down and wait for college football, which is corporate enough for me.

MONDAY, AUGUST 29, 2011

A Visit with Dooley

Buddy Dooley dropped by my pad over the weekend. A mercurial character, you never know what will happen with Buddy when his dander is raised. He reminds me of one of those stuffed toys with a tiny motor in it that your sister had when you were growing up. Wind it up, set it on the floor, and watch it run in circles like a cat chasing its own tail.

Dooley brought along a few micro brews, his rustic old tape player, and we talked.

BD: Testing…testing 1, 2, 3…

TS: You should invest in a new player. Go digital, high tech. What kind of beer did you bring?

BD: Never mind the beer. If I decide you should have a beer you may have a beer. If I decide you are not deserving of a beer you will not have a beer.

TS: You're a tough character, Dooley.

BD: That is correct. How are things in the imperium, Simons? The holy world of publishing? It's good to see you are not dead or incapacitated in any noticeable way. We haven't talked in weeks. What's new, pussycat?

TS: Jesus…

BD: Speaking of which. What do you think of Gov. Rick Perry? Makin' a run? He gonna win it?

TS: I think he and Bachmann will start an affair on the campaign trail. In a huge October surprise the media will reveal Michele and Rick share an affinity for bondage and kinky sex. The story will break on TMZ. Romney will slide in. Obama will rout him in the G.E.

BD: Do you like Obama?

TS: No. Next question.

BD: Is he worse than Dubya?

TS: Same horse. Different color.

BD: Quite.

TS: I do think many racists in the US hate Obama for all the wrong reasons. They hate him because he's half black. He was born in Kenya, right? They're torn, though. The hate is sometimes eclipsed by their love because he assassinated bin Laden. And Americans, particularly the right, love assassination. But the far right is nervous. The black revolution is playing out in their feverish dreams. It's odd, but recall that these people are revisionist crazies. For many, everything progressive that has happened since Ozzie and Harriet were on TV has been just plain wrong. Civil rights. The war on poverty. Feminism. Sexual equality. Gay marriage. You name it. Not to over-generalize or anything.

BD: Who is a bigger threat to liberty—Bachmann or Perry?

TS: They're both dangerous. But let's not talk about this. This is depressing. Thing is the world was never the way these people imagine it in the first place. This really isn't worth discussing in my opinion.

BD: Sexier? Bachmann or Palin?

TS: Dooley… Are you going there?

BD: Don't tell me you wouldn't.

TS: Give me a beer, you idiot.

(I was surprised here. Buddy shared his beer without protest.)

TS: (smacking my lips) Aaaaaah. Curve Ball Blonde Ale. Good stuff.

BD: Moving on to the press, TS...

TS: A good year, Buddy. A real good year. Had some good help, excellent advice, made deals with three highly accomplished writers who jumped on board. The press has legitimacy now, driven by quality work that people who give a damn about books will notice. I'm convinced of that. Over time, this work will stick out. We'll be discovered. The press, I mean. The writers are already known. I'm proud and pleased they came aboard. It's a nice fit. The world will catch up one day.

BD: And they are...

TS: The Deemer brothers, Bill and Charles, and K.C. Bacon. All three brought it, delivered the goods. Better than I imagined it could be.

BD: How's your novel going?

TS: Not quite as well, BD. I gave it to a good reader, a solid critic. He tore it apart. I'll take his word for it. Writing a novel is the hardest goddamn thing to do. Even a passable one. Mine needs a lot of work. Eventually, I'll get going on it again, from scratch quite possibly. A complete re-write.

That's what it needs. But I'm not overly worried about it. If it comes, fine. If not I won't shoot myself like Hem or Hunter. That would be a waste and a grand delusion. Those guys were great writers. I don't match up with their prose, and I don't own a shotgun.

BD: Anything else cookin'?

TS: I'm planning a book with Charles Lucas, the ceramic artist, photographer and painter. He is working hard, getting his images just right for an art book. We'll see. I don't have a deadline or anything. It's Round Bend, Buddy, a work-in-progress and the establishment of a legacy. This is for friends, family, and the historians. The work can't stop. If the public picks up on it, hooray!

BD: Well, you do indeed make it sound important. I understand you are a football fan.

TS: I am. I'll admit it.

BD: Are you going to get naked now and charge me out of the three-point stance like that drunk kid at Oregon State who charged the police?

TS: That kid transferred to one of the Montana schools. State, I believe.

BD: Fit in there I guess. Have you ever drove a car at 118 MPH in a speed trap between Albany and Eugene and gotten away with it?

TS: Ninety-nine, until the wheels went wobbly and I figured I'd better back off. Didn't see a cop. One didn't evidently see me, either. Another time, I raced from San Jose to Eugene with some friends. We picked cars up at an auction in San Jose and drove hard through the night back to Eugene. Nearly died in the Siskiyou Mountains. Had a little drift, fishtailed somewhat. Car was gutless. By the time I moved to New England in 1974 I had that stuff out of my system.

BD: Is Chipper Kelly on the up and up?

TS: Is college football corrupt?

BD: Hmmmm… You're a bit much at times, TS. Do you admire Phil Knight?

TS: Buddy, I can feel you egging me on. Are you looking for a fight?

BD: Before you get all pissy, tell me something…

TS: Sure, Dooley.

BD: Do you expect me to give you another beer?

(click)

MONDAY, OCTOBER 11, 2010

Violent Sports

Except for a few rough spots, I thought my Round Bend Hour went fairly well yesterday. I tend to lose my flow of conversation, partly because I still have a microphone phobia, and partly because I ain't that good of a talker to begin with.

With that in mind, maybe this is a very odd thing for me to try to accomplish.

However, I feel there has been some improvement in my voice, phrasing, and tech expertise. Still a ways off, but hell, I love doing it.

If the folks at http://houseofsound.org/ will keep me on I'll plug away, always expecting to get better.

It is a blast.

Speaking of hard hits--I was really concerned when Oregon's Kenjon Barner went down in the game at Pullman Saturday. You hate seeing that kind of thing. But at the same time you know it happens, will happen, and has happened. Football is violent. I equate it with the "sweet science," boxing. When the performance is right, it is a thing of beauty, like Ali dancing in the ring and throwing flurries, or like Barner before his injury, running an end around and picking up graceful yards.

I've seen two fights on television that ended in death. I watched as Emile Griffith killed Benny "Kid" Paret, and I watched three decades later when Ray "Boom Boom" Mancini killed Duk Koo Kim.

A sad, sad part of the game.

SATURDAY, OCTOBER 9, 2010

Highs and Lows

Damn near everything is perfect except the weather here today. It is raining. As a native son, I should be used to it by now, but I've never liked it.

I'd rather be a sun ray than a raindrop, Buddy Dooley says, espousing his naïve New Age mentality and causing me to consider punching him in the nose.

The day is perfect because I feel pretty good. I feel alive, which isn't always the case. It never is for one with a sizable streak of morbidity running in his blood. It's perfect because it's the right day for football, with a lineup of interesting games this afternoon. I'm actually looking forward to seeing OSU and Arizona play. I'll root for OSU.

I'll take in the Oregon game as well, the idolater that I am.

There may be just one troubling situation brewing. A guy I have completely disassociated myself from is organizing a Wake for my friend Roger, who died six-months ago. I can't in good conscience go, knowing how disrespectful this guy could be toward Roger at times. He is a self-aggrandizer of the highest (lowest?) caliber, and I really don't want to hear him muddy up the record with his bullshit. A third party is arguing with me about my decision, which is irritating. Show some understanding for god's sake!

FRIDAY, AUGUST 24, 2012

Another View

Charles Deemer, the former star quarterback/safety/punter of the Cal Tech freshman football team, takes me to task here for my ecstatic preview of the upcoming college football season.

Wherein he recycles his usual bag of neurotic tropes against the game:

Nike is evil and the University of Oregon is now Nike U., run by the malevolent and despicable Oregon alum Phil Knight, whom Deemer once interviewed and found disagreeable. Also a Stanford Business School graduate, Knight has famously endowed that fine university as well as the University of Oregon. He is also known to have put up the cash so that Oregon State University could keep its excellent baseball coach, Pat Casey.

Corporate patronage exists in the university system? I had no idea.

Let's focus on the real issue in plain sight here. The endowment/patronage system, coupled with increasingly high tuition costs at every university in the land, is creating a new class of permanently impoverished former college students with mountains of debt and limited opportunities for advancement. That system aids two elements within the structural makeup of the education hierarchy: Bankers and college administrators. The very notion that in order to "succeed" in life one is required to accumulate massive debt is a cruel joke being played on everybody.

It is better to have a rich uncle named Sam. The merit system is all but dead because there are too many bright, unemployed people out there and too few good jobs.

The nation needs more poor intellectuals like it needs another hole in its head. Perhaps one advantage that may come from this, likely long after I am buried and forgotten is that the disenfranchised intellectuals will rise up one day and seize control of the instruments of power. Education along with health care will become available for all and not just for the privileged.

Corruption is rife in college football. I agree. It is also rife in Congress. I'm more worried about Congress than I am the simple-minded game of football, which after all is merely an entertainment. We are possibly losing the fight against corruption on an enormous scale, one that matters, and one that causes our worries about mere games to pale. Corruption is everywhere. There is no getting around it.

To eradicate the corruption in big-time college football the designers and funding bodies of all our institutions must first deal with the grieving spirit of the body politic. All of it is linked to the almighty dollar.

Football is a gnat on a fly's ass, in other words. It is sitting in the third-class section of the collective flight to ruin that is the corruption inherent in the flailing U.S. Empire.

Well, I can be a generalist, too.

* Dancing in the end zone upsets Deemer. He apparently doesn't realize that dance steps have been outlawed in college football for years now. To dance is to be penalized and draw the wrath of the head coach, never mind the player's position coach. The corrupt NCAA made that rule in case you are interested.

Oh, how players today would love to dance if they could.

*The "thugs" versus "character" issue in college football is an interesting one, albeit rife with racial overtones. There are thousands of college football players in the U.S. I don't have a clue as to how many are thugs or how many are "character guys." I read the sports pages and see that players, year in and year, out get arrested for a variety of criminal behaviors. Many, particularly recently, are kicked off their teams.

I don't read much about the upstanding guys in college football because they're seldom written about. I do recall a story awhile back about Oregon's John Boyett volunteer-mentoring in his hometown high school every summer, so I know there is at least one character guy at Oregon.

Bless us.

Deemer has an issue with the student/athlete and sees a landscape wherein the athlete is perhaps getting a free pass academically. I've been to college. I've seen many students who failed to grease their academic wheels. Few of them were athletes, perhaps because the numbers were disparate, but most failed because they were too immature to study and take academic training seriously. In my own case, I nearly flunked out the year I played college football at a small Oregon school. I'm absolutely certain this was because I didn't apply myself to the work.

I eventually made things right.

At the University of Oregon, I watched a trust-fund kid or two flunk out, laughing all the way.

As for Deemer's constant comparison of futbol and football (soccer and American football), I'd like to say that I too think soccer is a wonderful sport, though the American Major League Soccer organization is another cruel joke. Millions around the world can't be wrong about soccer, particularly those in the traditional soccer nations.

Soccer, however, is only remotely related to American football and should be part of a separate discussion. All they have in common is the name football and eleven players per side.

Postscript: Jingoism, Yellow Ribbons and American Sports

I turned 40 the day the U.S. began its first bombing campaign against Saddam Hussein's Baghdad, January 16, 1991.

As it happened, I was scheduled to leave the next day for Long Beach Peninsula in Washington State. I planned to live a solitary month in a trailer rental there and work on a couple of writing projects.

If you're old enough, you'll remember that the first Gulf War was a television bonanza for CNN, with its cast of Pentagon experts and sexy reporters giving viewers their first taste of life in wartime as a 24/7 news event.

Vietnam is often referred to as America's first televised war, but its coverage was light-hearted compared to the news/hyperbole CNN floated in Gulf War I. The black and white imagery of annihilation, video shot from thousands of feet above the intended target, sanitized death—it was all there for the transfixed and undiscerning viewer.

Then there appeared the helicopter shots of the "Highway of Death," a sort of media dessert—graphic images of the destruction of Hussein's retreating forces, along with many civilians caught up in the carnage.

I caught glimpses of the coverage in a Seaview, Wash. bar near my trailer each evening before trudging back to work, usually in a dismal mood. Back in my trailer those nights, I didn't work on my planned projects, but wrote an anti-war play instead, which I titled simply, The War.

I was listening to the OPB affiliate out of Astoria, Oregon one night when the airwaves went silent. The broadcaster working that night was righteously lambasting the war; he suddenly quit his job and walked away from his microphone, muttering that he couldn't take any more.

I feared for his career in radio, but I admired his bold move.

Weeks earlier, I had dutifully protested the coming war, marching along with thousands of others through Portland's streets. As with every anti-war march since the Vietnam era, I knew what effect protest would have on U.S. militarism—none.

I was reconciled to living with that knowledge forever while using protest as a symbol.

However, once the Gulf War began I was surprised by the depth of the jingoism and mindless sloganeering of the pro-war crowd as the U.S. commenced its slaughter. Given events of the ensuing years, I of course now realize I shouldn't have been surprised, but at the time I thought our citizenry had transcended such nonsense.

Then I realized that for half the nation the scars of the Vietnam era had faded away or never existed. The citizenry was ripe for another dose of poison as propaganda.

The divisiveness of U.S. war policy had returned with a vengeance.

Out came the flags and yellow ribbons and bumper stickers in 1991, along with the "support-our-troops" messaging sent directly to the anti-war crowd:

"We do not protest against America. We love America more than you do."

Here it is 25-years later and Colin Kaepernick can't say what is on his mind without many in the jingoistic, flag-waving American sports crowd climbing all over him.

I think my instincts are correct about this. Americans have "shrank out of sight," to quote Mark Twain's *War Prayer*, too often in the face of their government's wars.

Kaepernick seems to be in agreement. I admire his willingness to say something about the obvious. Jocks don't do that often enough. With one small protest CK transcended the ordinary.

***

Something is happening now, though. The debate has opened up. NFL players and the owners are talking about race. That can be a good thing, and hopefully it will lead to change and a larger understanding of what Kaepernick brought to the fore with his protest.

There have been others who broke the code of racial silence in the history of professional sports, but they are few. The sixties were particularly volatile in that regard. CK is just the latest to test the repercussions of dissent. Asked about his protest's potential negative effect on his career, he said, "I don't care."

***

Professional sports are filled with knuckleheads. I recall Luke Scott, when he was a Baltimore Oriole, allowing that he didn't believe, back in the glorious hours of the birther movement, that President Obama is a U.S. citizen.

As I've attempted to convey here, I was once an enthusiastic jock myself. As I've also related, I didn't always fit in with the athletes in my cohort because my views have long been somewhat left of centerfield.

What had happened in Luke Scott's case is that someone lobbed Scottie a few political questions regarding our president and the ball hit him on the forehead before he juggled and then dropped it.

I once sat in Portland's Multnomah Stadium (now soccer-dedicated Providence Park) during a Portland Beavers baseball game, the summer of 1980, and quietly received the taunts of the entire bullpen of the Phoenix Giants as I remained seated during the playing of the national anthem.

Here is what I have in common with Kaepernick. Sitting out the anthem has been a long-time habit of mine, and my business, as I've long resisted the way sports and politics enmesh in our society, an embarrassing jingoistic tendency.

By the time the warbling, awful singer finished mangling the ugly song, the pitchers were threatening to come into the stands and kick my ass.

The Soviets had recently invaded Afghanistan and Jimmy Carter had called off U.S. participation in the Moscow Olympics in protest. U.S. nationalism and the most naïve kind of American patriotism had a grip on the reactionaries among us.

I waved at the bullpen heroes and put on my best smile. Didn't they know they should have been paying attention to the anthem and not clamoring so viciously for my head?

I thought they were being most disrespectful—to the flag, and the poor singer!

Can I relate to Colin Kaepernick's protest? Of course I can.

About the Author

Terry Simons is the founder of Round Bend Press Books and the blog, Round Bend Press Detritus. He has worked as a day laborer, dishwasher, factory drone, community organizer, journalist, media consultant and freelance writer. He attended the University of Oregon and Portland State University, where he read journalism, politics, literature and history. He is the author most recently of "Along Came the Death Squad: Political and Scattered Notes." Round Bend Press books are available from Amazon.

Contact: roundbendpressbooks@yahoo.com

www.ingramcontent.com/pod-product-compliance
Lightning Source LLC
Chambersburg PA
CBHW060507090426
42735CB00011B/2142